# INSIDER'S GUIDE TO Compliance

*Real World Advice for Building a Successful Compliance Program*

SUSAN LEE WALBERG, JD MPA CHC

Insider's Guide to Compliance



For information about this title or to order other books and/or electronic media, contact the publisher:
Compliance Ala Carte
swalberg@compliancealacarte.com

978-0-9998605-0-2 (print)
978-0-9998605-1-9 (eBook)

Printed in the United States of America

Nothing in this book is intended to constitute legal advice.

# CONTENTS

# INTRODUCTION

Welcome to the *Insider's Guide to Compliance.* As an introduction, I would like to put this book in context as to what it is and what it is not. Many technical resources are available to new healthcare compliance officers, which I reference throughout. This handbook is not intended to replace those publications but is meant to be a supplement. This book provides insights and real-world tips for compliance officers who are just starting out. Although my focus is on health care, many of the issues and suggestions herein could apply in other settings as well.

I have spent my entire career—more years than I care to admit—working as a compliance professional in this field. I have worked for health plans, hospitals, health systems, Centers for Medicare and Medicaid Services (CMS) subcontractors, and pretty much every type of healthcare provider. I've worked as an in-house attorney and as a compliance officer. I have worked on fraud and abuse audits and investigations and in building compliance programs. I have watched this profession change from a manual on the shelf to an integral part of organizational leadership. Through these experiences, I have identified patterns, recurring issues, and a host of areas that are commonly misunderstood or mishandled.

This handbook will walk you through the elements of a compliance program, but it is not meant to be a recitation of what you need to do to build each element. Instead, I provide key pointers on how to implement each of the requirements based on my practical experience. This book is not intended to be simplistic, or to minimize the criticality of the compliance officer's role. In fact, I believe this is such an important position that I want to help those starting out by lending some insights and suggestions to simplify what has become an increasingly complex responsibility.

If I were to sit down with a new compliance officer, maybe over a glass of wine after a long day at a conference, what I would tell this person makes up the content of this book. I advise any new compliance officers to become acquainted with two resources: first, the Health and Human Services Office of Inspector General (OIG) website, which contains many guidance documents that form the basis of compliance programs for health care and provides detailed reviews of specific functional areas within health care, which can be a very useful starting point; and second, the Health Care Compliance Association (HCCA), which is a great resource with many available materials and conferences.

Other organizations, as well, are useful and provide tools, training, and certifications. Go look around online and talk to other compliance officers, if you know any, and you will discover a wealth of information.

With that said, I hope you enjoy this handbook; it is intended to be easy to read as well as useful and informative.

# PART I

# THE FUNDAMENTALS

# PRELIMINARY MATTERS

Compliance programs are based on the "seven elements," as outlined by the various Health and Human Services Office of Inspector General (OIG) guidance documents. The OIG guidance is derived from the United States Sentencing Commission *Guidelines Manual* (hereafter referred to as U.S. Sentencing Guidelines), which provides an outline of factors that can help an organization reduce its penalties if it is found to have violated applicable laws and regulations. It is useful to be familiar with the U.S. Sentencing Guidelines and to understand those standards as the basis for compliance programs, particularly when you are educating governing boards and leadership teams about the genesis and importance of compliance programs.

The U.S. Sentencing Guidelines contain guidance relating to all types of criminal activity; the chapter on sentencing of organizations includes discussion of an effective compliance and ethics program. The U.S. Sentencing Guidelines do not, themselves, provide much detail about each of the seven elements, but rather defer to industry standards. These industry standards continue to develop, in large part through the OIG guidance documents. One example of changes is the addition of risk assessments as an element of an effective program. Some outlines of compliance programs include this element, and others do not; I include it here because it is a critical part of not only identifying risk, but also planning and making your program meaningful and effective.

### *Are Compliance Programs Voluntary?*

In the beginning, when the OIG Guidance for healthcare compliance programs was published, compliance programs in the healthcare arena were voluntary and recommended as best practice. Over time, they became "industry standard," but remained voluntary. Because programs were considered voluntary, some organizations did not see the value in compliance programs and did not want to invest in them.

During the voluntary phase, I was often asked about return on investment, or the ROI, of establishing a compliance program. Organizations wanted me to quantify the costs and benefits. Some organizations were willing to risk the potential expense of compliance violations as a cost of doing business. I recall one instance, in particular, when I was explaining a regulatory requirement to a finance executive. The executive looked at me and said, "No, this isn't cost-effective. We are not going to do that." And that was it. This viewpoint is aligned with the "fix it going forward" perspective, which was a common view of leaders and managers who believed this was an adequate way of addressing identified problems.

When the Deficit Reduction Act of 2005 (DRA) was passed, the landscape began to change. This law required, among other things, that organizations with Medicaid revenues in excess of $5 million have a compliance program. It also required those organizations to provide clear guidance to employees and business partners about the federal False Claims Act. As part of the DRA, states were motivated to pass false claims acts that mirrored the federal law in order to secure federal money for Medicaid programs.

From my perspective, at this point compliance programs were no longer voluntary, although smaller organizations could certainly argue that they didn't meet the threshold. To me, the government's expectation was pretty clear, and it was not a good idea to devise excuses to avoid putting such a program in place. I wouldn't want to be the person who has to explain to the federal government why I don't have to have a compliance program. It just wouldn't send a good message about my organization.

Enter the Affordable Care Act (ACA) of 2010. Regardless of the various disputes over "Obamacare," this law reiterates the government's expectations about compliance programs. Sections 6102 and 6401 of the ACA state that skilled nursing facilities (SNFs) and nursing facilities (NFs) and other healthcare providers enrolled in Medicare, Medicaid, and the Children's Health Insurance Program adopt compliance programs as a condition of enrollment. One could debate the true intent and meaning of the language; but again, it is clear what the government wants to see in place. Whether or not actual regulations are issued that require specific elements, the expectation is clear and the industry guidance is available.

Would you really want to try to tell the government why you don't need a compliance program and why you don't have to have one? Sometimes people get so caught up in parsing the language of the law to make an argument that they miss the big picture, which, in this case, is that the government expects healthcare organizations to have compliance programs. To argue that you don't have to have one is tantamount to saying you don't really care to invest in ensuring your organization follows the laws and regulations appropriately. Not an argument I would be comfortable making.

So, are compliance programs voluntary? No. Not anymore.

### *Who Should Be the Compliance Officer?*

No single professional background is most suitable for the role of compliance officer, although opinions differ, and answers may vary depending on the organization. Some people believe compliance officers should be attorneys; some believe a coder or billing person is best; and others like to see a certified public accountant (CPA) or internal audit expert running the compliance function. Still others lean toward other professional backgrounds, such as nursing.

The truth is that healthcare compliance has become so complex that one specific background is not going to cover all areas of necessary expertise. For instance, an attorney is well equipped to analyze laws and regulations and certainly can manage investigations and do policy development and reviews. But most attorneys are not qualified to conduct documentation and coding reviews. Conversely, a coder can do coding reviews but may not have the skills to analyze financial arrangements. Auditors are proficient at identifying and quantifying compliance risks, and are comfortable with conducting compliance audits and assessments, but may not be as experienced with sensitive human resources (HR) compliance matters. Because quality of care is now part of the landscape for compliance, medical necessity is a significant compliance issue that has been the focus of many government investigations and settlements. Who is better at working on medical necessity cases than someone with a clinical background? That person might, however, struggle with designing a robust contract review process.

It is important to recognize that the various backgrounds bring their own biases, skills, and perspectives. An attorney may focus on regulatory policies but may not have a solid understanding of operational issues and challenges that hamper the organization's ability to comply with well-intentioned policies crafted by counsel. A coder might think of coding as being compliance. A clinician focuses on the patient care perspective, which, of course, is ultimately what health care is all about. But it is not that simple, not anymore.

When you start out in compliance, and realize the full scope of your responsibilities, you might be overwhelmed by all the types of issues that come under your purview. The complexity of the compliance function is the reason why the compliance officer must have access to other resources from the various areas of expertise, which we will get to shortly. The main idea is for the individual in the compliance role to understand the full scope of what a compliance program includes and to have the organizational support to make it happen.

The biggest mistake organizations make in selecting a compliance officer is not choosing a person with the wrong skill set, but rather picking just anyone in the organization and assigning compliance to that individual. Organizations that do this are usually coming at it from a "check the box" perspective. The individual who is assigned the role of compliance officer then sets about trying to figure out what to do, and soon discovers that there is a lot to learn and that compliance is not a simple matter.

Dealing with the complexity of the role, as well as compliance itself, is challenging for someone who has never done it before. Not only do newbies have to learn the role, but they have to teach the organization's leadership what the job entails and what it requires in terms of support and resources. In an organization that doesn't understand compliance, that simply assigns compliance oversight to someone in order to check it off the list, you can be sure that getting additional resources is not going to be a simple matter for the new compliance officer.

Sometimes compliance is assigned as an add-on duty to an existing full-time role. Organizations often do this to demonstrate they have a compliance program and to satisfy the requirement without actually having to put any effort or resources into it. In a small practice this makes sense, because a small practice might not have the resources to hire a full-time compliance officer, which would really be overkill. Larger organizations, however, run into trouble when they tack compliance on to an employee's existing job.

If you take a look, the OIG's Corporate Integrity Agreements (CIAs) require that compliance officers have no other duties that interfere with their ability to devote their time to compliance. Assigning compliance as an added responsibility is also unfair to the compliance officer. If there is a government audit or investigation, the compliance officer will undoubtedly get thrown under the bus for not doing the job properly, when, in fact, there was no way this person could meet all the requirements of a compliance officer in addition to the duties of the other full-time role.

The positions most often assigned compliance as an add-on responsibility are those in risk management, quality improvement, human resources, health information management, coding, and billing. As you can imagine, these are full-time jobs with plenty of demanding work to fill the day without responsibility for another critical program, too.

If you are the person to whom compliance has been assigned in addition to your usual duties, my word of advice is to understand the difficulty of trying to meet both (or all) sets of responsibilities and to be prepared to ask for additional resources. That said, one individual can *oversee* more than one area. For example, risk managers can oversee compliance; they just can't be expected to complete all the tasks of both roles without help. Make sure you grasp the functions of your dual roles well enough to be able to teach them to staff and then delegate and evaluate.

Be prepared for the challenge of explaining your roles to leadership. In many instances, leaders don't understand the difference, for example, between risk management and compliance. Or why the coding manager can't readily assume the compliance officer role. For many leaders, the delineation between roles is very blurry; it's not their background and not their primary focus. So, just be ready to articulate the differences in positions and what each role demands in order for it to be accomplished successfully.

We have talked about who can be a compliance officer. Now let's discuss who should *not*. A chief financial officer should never be designated as the compliance officer. Those two roles combined present a conflict of interest or, at a minimum, give the appearance of a conflict, and the government takes a very dim view of this arrangement.

Another no-no is having general counsel act as the compliance officer. This one is not as clear-cut, and it's even more of a gray area in smaller organizations. For larger organizations, however, there is no question that Legal and Compliance functions should be separate. The OIG provides plenty of opinions on this matter: any CIA with an organization in which Compliance reports to Legal will require that reporting structure to be changed. The compliance officer should have a significant level of autonomy, and ideally reports to both the chief executive officer and the board or board committee.

The bottom line is that the "perfect" compliance officer matches no specific profile as far as background or skill set, but does require organizational support, adequate resources, and freedom from any appearance of a conflict of interest or conflict in roles. This person also needs to be eager to learn—because in this role there is always something new!

# PROGRAM STRUCTURE

IF YOUR ORGANIZATION ends up under the microscope, one thing the government will look at is compliance program structure. It wants to see that the compliance officer has direct lines to the board, or a committee of the board, and to the chief executive officer. This doesn't mean that structures other than this can't work or pass muster. But certain limitations on structuring the compliance program apply, as I mentioned before and describe more fully here.

The compliance officer cannot also be the chief financial officer or report to the CFO. This structure might be the biggest mistake an organization can make. There is an inherent conflict of interest between the compliance officer and the CFO that could prevent the compliance officer from being independent and effective. For instance, as the compliance officer, say you conduct an audit and discover that a certain service has been routinely billed with a modifier that increases reimbursement. You need to figure out how prevalent the issue is by doing a more comprehensive audit, and then you will have to refund the overpayment to the government and other payers as applicable.

On the other hand, it is the job of the CFO to protect the organization's coffers. I'm not saying CFOs are dishonest, or that they would not allow you to do the right and necessary thing. What I am saying is that it could be more difficult for you as the compliance officer if your boss is tasked with saving money. Not only is there the appearance of a conflict of interest, but also it could generate scrutiny by the government after you submit the overpayment. When the government sees that the compliance officer reports to the CFO, it would (rightly) question whether you are allowed to properly do your job. There is a natural tension between Compliance and Finance, although most organizations don't have an actual conflict between the two because individuals in both departments understand their roles and responsibilities, creating a natural system of checks and balances. But this structure still raises a question and is not an advisable arrangement.

A variety of opinions have been written about the compliance officer reporting to general counsel. As I mentioned before, the OIG frowns on this arrangement, citing the different perspectives and priorities of the two roles. Although it is less intuitive than the conflict with the CFO, it is more likely to be seen (by leadership) as a good fit in organizations, and more opinions have been written about the relationship for that reason.

The role of the compliance officer is to identify, prevent, and detect legal, regulatory, and ethical violations. The compliance officer is also responsible for disclosing those same violations if appropriate. Legal counsel is tasked with defending the organization and providing guidance when issues such as self-disclosures arise. These roles obviously overlap, and are not directly in conflict, but they do approach the subject from different perspectives. It is important that both the compliance officer and general counsel have access to leadership and the board, and that they work together in a collaborative, not dominant-subordinate, relationship. I have known wonderful general counsels I wouldn't hesitate to work for as a compliance officer, despite all the industry warnings to the contrary. I have also encountered some who definitely shouldn't be running Compliance, because they want to keep compliance problems under wraps and have interfered with open disclosure to the board.

Politics also plays a huge role in the compliance officer's positioning in the food chain. Although many organizations are coming to recognize the compliance officer as part of the leadership team, still others understand the responsibilities of the function poorly and do not value the role. I once saw an administrative assistant named as the compliance officer. Such individuals do not know the compliance role, and neither do they have authority or standing in the organization. Can you imagine an administrative assistant informing a chief of surgery that he or she will be audited? No, I didn't think so. Administrative assistants certainly wouldn't report in at board meetings. It is challenging enough for a compliance officer to assert authority in a political environment where egos swell and turf wars abound without being at the bottom of the pecking order to boot.

The fact is, some organizations just don't want to give the compliance officer much authority. They may not really understand the role, or they may fear the idea of a "police" function with too much clout ruffling feathers and causing trouble. In a hospital, for instance, the executive leaders don't want their key physicians complaining about some "upstart" compliance officer coming into their unit and reviewing their records. Physicians may feel it disrupts their practice or that the individual has no right or qualifications to be interfering in their business. In either event, executives are concerned about running their hospital and keeping their physicians happy.

What leaders all need to understand, however, is that the compliance officer actually serves to help them and to keep them out of trouble, not to cause problems. This is the crux of the compliance officer's challenge, and sometimes it can take a long time and a lot of skill to overcome.

So, once the compliance officer is positioned in the right structure, reporting to the CEO and the board, how is that person able to manage compliance across so many different functional areas? I will use a hospital as an example, although most healthcare organizations perform a variety of services that also call for different skill sets or expertise. In a hospital, the compliance officer should be involved in compliance matters related to accurate coding and billing. Maybe the compliance officer isn't a coder and has never dropped a bill. As I said earlier, there's no requirement that compliance officers have any specific background or expertise, but that person does need to be able to ensure that the coding and billing functions are operating in compliance with applicable regulatory requirements and that the functions are being monitored and objectively audited on a routine basis.

What about Human Resources? Many laws relate to how employees are managed, such as fair labor standards, discrimination, and so forth. Unions in the house add another layer of complexity. Say, for instance, the compliance officer is a coder by background. How can that compliance officer possibly be an HR expert and evaluate a complaint that accuses HR of violating wage and hour laws? It's possible, of course, but probably not a common area of strength for a coder.

Those examples are not at all far-fetched. It's all in a day's work. This dilemma of covering the range of expertise needed to properly run Compliance leads to the other aspect of effective compliance program structure, which is the Compliance Committee.

The operational Compliance Committee is an expected part of compliance programs, according to any industry guidance that discusses program structure. So how do you set up a Compliance Committee, and who should participate? Keep in mind that this may be more challenging than you might expect. People are busy and are probably already on more committees than they like. Going to meetings gets in the way of doing "real" work.

Despite any objections, it is critical the Compliance Committee includes a good cross section of representation, and the individuals selected should have a respectable level of authority in their functional area. They don't all have to be C-suite people, but they should rank high enough in the organization that they can speak for their functional area.

The CFO should be on the committee but may designate a vice president or some other finance leader instead. That's okay, but I wouldn't typically accept a financial analyst, for example, who isn't at a level to represent Finance. Human Resources must be at the table, as does the business office. You should have at least one physician, someone in Risk Management, Health Information Management (HIM), Nursing, and the chief operating officer. If the compliance officer isn't the privacy officer, then the privacy officer is an integral part of the group, as is the chief information security officer. And don't forget general counsel! Look at the leaders in the organization and identify any key areas that should also be included, based on the nature of the organization and how it's structured.

The reason for including this array of perspectives should be clear: The compliance officer isn't an expert in all these areas. Not only that, but the members of the Compliance Committee help the compliance program achieve buy-in across the organization. The committee also puts its weight behind approving bodies of work or policies, which takes the burden off the individual compliance officer and makes it clear that decisions are made with the right level of input and authority.

Having many perspectives on the committee is also hugely beneficial in terms of developing policies and procedures. As mentioned earlier, how could someone with a coding background create a contract approval checklist for lease arrangements? Of course, the individual can research and learn the topic, but the tool will be more readily accepted after it has been reviewed and approved by the committee, which includes people from Legal and Finance.

How can you get the right people to give up their time, absent a command from above? (Which you can get if necessary. If you can't get that support from your leadership, you have other problems.) One strategy is to help potential Compliance Committee members understand that you want to ensure that you write policies that work for their operational areas. People live in fear of "Corporate" or the C-suite devising mandates that are operational nightmares. This fear is not irrational; it is learned. Be very aware of this overarching apprehension, and use it to leverage people to work with you.

The other strategy is appealing to people's pride in their work. Make sure they understand that their perspective is critical to compliance program success because you are not the expert on human resources, finance, or whatever area they oversee. It's flattery, to be sure, but it's also the truth. When you are humble and sincere, asking for help is much more effective than trying to command people to participate.

This Compliance Committee should meet at least quarterly. I recommend that you establish an expectation that if you circulate an item in between meetings, members will look it over and provide feedback or input if requested. This keeps your work from getting log-jammed and is a particularly good idea for when you are dealing with potentially controversial policies. Conflicts of interest and gifts are good examples of topics that can create friction. If you send one of these documents around just prior to the meeting when it will be discussed, potentially you will encounter all the blow-back in the meeting and will have to then go back and do major rewrites. Not to mention how unpleasant it can be to get dressed down in the meeting for not putting more effort on the front end!

In one organization early in my career, I revised an existing Code of Conduct and tightened up the standards related to gifts. I dutifully called a meeting of all the key stakeholders to solicit input. But I hadn't circulated the proposed policies to all the attendees in advance, and a brawl nearly erupted in the meeting as two executives with strongly opposing views got into it over the appropriateness of certain gifts! Lesson learned.

It is far better to circulate documents well in advance, and ask each person for his or her thoughts on what might be problematic or what might be missing. I like to ask my key stakeholders individually, rather than in a note to everyone. When you approach them individually, they understand that you are asking them, specifically, and will feel more valued as well as less able to ignore you. They are more likely to be candid, as well, if they have particular concerns about the issue. Trust me on this: I have learned some interesting news by approaching people one on one. I have also been ignored when I failed to do so.

So, if you get your key people to weigh in early, you can then circulate a better-polished document and have some people at the table who are already advocates because they helped create it. It may seem like an obvious strategy, but you'd be surprised. Keeping in contact with the committee members between meetings saves you a lot of time in the long run, too, because the approval process should proceed more quickly.

One more note: You will quickly learn who is not a big supporter of Compliance during this process. Shocking, I know.

My advice is to put extra effort into getting to know your detractors and their respective areas of expertise. Then make those individuals a close adviser, if you can. This is a political move, but a very effective one. It typically silences your biggest detractors and may even convert them into supporters once they feel ownership of what you're doing. I've seen it work over and over. It's basic human psychology: You can't hate something if you helped build it.

Don't feel that you have to identify these individuals right away; it is best to really get to know the power structure, not only those with the "real" power, but also those with the power of influence. Not all big mouths are good resources for you to develop. You need to figure out their actual level of expertise and how respected, feared, or both they are in the organization. Those people with real influence who hate Compliance or feel threatened by your role are the ones to target. Look at it as a challenge. It's very rewarding to overcome opposition, and you can almost always do it if you manage it correctly. Respect their knowledge, stay humble, and ask for their help ... and see what happens. Sometimes it happens quickly and sometimes not, but usually it happens.

Another option relating to your program structure is the use of liaisons who work in different functional areas. The liaison is not a full-time compliance role, but rather a contact person for various units. For departments that have very specific regulatory requirements, or that represent high-risk areas, it is very useful to have a compliance point person to coordinate education, monitoring efforts, regulatory updates, and so forth. Examples of departments where this is helpful are Coding, Billing, Medical Records, Pharmacy, Lab, and Research. For a health system, the liaison may be a full-time position, particularly if there is a business office. If there are designated compliance officers or directors in these areas, make sure they at least have a dotted line to you if your role is at the corporate level.

It may sound obvious, but I have seen situations where this was not the case, and coordination was much more complicated. Think, for instance, of annual work planning. If a business office compliance officer reports to the vice president or the CFO, this individual may have an entirely different idea of what the annual work plan should look like. This arrangement can be difficult to navigate, politically, and you will need to get the CEO to understand and assist if it's a problem.

Another structure issue that arises with some regularity relates to the merging of Compliance with other functions, such as Internal Audit or Quality. There is no reason why one person cannot be a leader for multiple functions such as these. Combining functions has some advantages, as well, if done with due deliberation. For instance, Internal Audit can coordinate risk assessment and work planning with Compliance, making sure that there isn't any overlap and that all key risk areas are covered. The two areas can do reviews together, too. For instance, a review of physician contracts can be a very large project in a sizable organization. But the two departments can divide up the tasks. For example, Compliance can review and document contract terms, and Internal Audit can audit payments made to physicians and compare them to contract terms.

Quality is another area where there is increasing synergy owing to changing reimbursement models and regulatory requirements that really merge the two areas. The "Two Midnights Rule" is a great example, in which physician admission decisions are subject to CMS regulations. The decision of admitting a patient to "inpatient" as opposed to "observation" status affects how the care is reimbursed, so CMS decided to put regulatory requirements around those decisions. This turns admitting and patient status decisions into compliance issues. Compliance officers should now have a seat at the table when operations meet to discuss admissions and readmissions. Things have changed, and organizations are now seeing the need for these areas to work closely together.

Reimbursement, as well, now is related to quality indicators, and this trend is not going away. Joint Commission accreditation aligns well with Compliance, as does Risk Management, particularly when it comes to root cause analyses, corrective action plans, and monitoring. These activities are conducted by all of the above functions and often overlap in terms of their impact.

The real question is not whether these areas can be aligned, but rather how to do it. Most important, make sure that each of these essential functions is adequately resourced. In the past, organizations have had a tendency to add compliance, patient safety, and Joint Commission accreditation to a quality director's or risk manager's duties. Although these roles are aligned, that does not mean that one individual can do them all.

It is possible to have an executive-level person lead multiple functions, but that person must be sure there is a dedicated person to run the quality program. Risk management, also, should not be an add-on. Compliance and privacy need to be staffed to adequately manage both programs, and even with entity-level or functional area compliance-privacy liaisons, there must be a leader who has time to focus on this role.

There is no single rule on how to set this up, so long as you remember that the government will look to see that the compliance officer isn't conflicted with multiple responsibilities. In reviewing various Corporate Integrity Agreements, the OIG is very clear about the compliance officer's freedom from conflicting responsibilities. Sometimes an arrangement might seem workable on paper but turns out otherwise; that's fine, as long as the organization is open to adding resources. If you are asked your opinion about one of these combining arrangements, you might want to do some homework, reach out to people in the functions in question, and come back with that information.

Leaders should have experience in all the areas they are overseeing. I'm a big believer in leaders who have actually done the job, because they can well understand the roles and how to mentor their staff. The reality, however, is that if you combine functions, it is unlikely that you will find someone with deep expertise in both areas. It's possible, but it's more likely that dual-role employees will have much greater strength in one area or the other. The organization must be mindful of this and provide appropriate resources and training to make sure that important functions are adequately managed.

One last item to cover with respect to structure: Privacy. It is not uncommon for Compliance and Privacy to be "owned" by the same person. I happen to think this makes sense because many of the activities, such as new employee orientation and annual education, can be done jointly. If the functions are separate, be very sure that there is close collaboration. My view is that Privacy should always have at least a dotted line to Compliance. There are so many efficiencies and synergies between the two functions, that for them to have completely different structures makes no sense. The compliance officer should always know about Privacy incidents and should be part of the mitigation response. So, depending on the size and structure of your organization, make sure to be closely aligned with Privacy.

Information Security, too, should be aligned with Compliance and Privacy. An experienced security officer is strong on the technical skills and understands the linkage with Privacy and Compliance. If Privacy and Information Security don't interact, there is a problem, because in the event of a breach, both functions need to be involved. Neither should be subordinate to the other, either. Privacy and Information Security require different sets of skills and knowledge and can help each other.

For example, in the area of policies and procedures, a highly technical person, such as someone in the Information Security function, may write abstract policies that normal employees won't understand, but the Privacy person can interpret the language and make the intent clear to users. Conversely, the security officer is the person who can best run access audits to verify whether an employee was inappropriately accessing a coworker's information. Their skill sets are complementary.

The bottom line is that these functions should collaborate, and even if none of them has a common reporting structure, they need to work together. Perhaps they form a small working group that meets monthly, as one possibility; but I warn against letting these functions exist in silos. At some point such a situation will create a problem.

Those are the key issues related to program structure. The OIG guidance documents do discuss key structural components of a compliance program, but keep in mind, a wide range of variation is acceptable.

# STANDARDS OF CONDUCT AND POLICIES

POLICIES ARE MY FAVORITE aspects of a compliance program because they are a way to make order out of chaos. Policies can be tricky, no doubt, especially in organizations that are policy-averse or highly political. I have seen one policy take two years to be passed by all the key stakeholders, and even that took nothing short of emotional manipulation. As I said earlier, many organizations don't like giving Compliance power or authority to own and enforce policies, particularly policies that cross into different functional areas where they are unwanted.

This perspective isn't entirely unreasonable: Nobody wants to be told how to do their job, especially by a person with no role in the functional unit. This is where relationships are supreme. As I go through the specific core policies later, I also advise you on who should be involved. This is more guidance that may seem self-evident, but you could be surprised. Some compliance officers do develop policies without ever discussing them with key stakeholders, and then they are shocked when there is a lot of pushback.

Creating policies on your own sets you up to be perceived as someone trying to assert authority over others in the organization, not as a team player. Most leaders do not find such maneuvering agreeable, and it's a great way to get people to complain about you to the CEO. Keep in mind, love for the compliance officer does not come naturally to many in an organization. We are seen as a necessary evil—some would argue about the *necessary* part.

A related challenge has to do with subject matter expertise, or lack thereof. If you are a new compliance officer, or even just new to the organization, you are not the expert on how every job is performed. You probably have a specific area of expertise and may lack knowledge in other areas. Let's take sanctions policies as an example. Sanctions policies identify the levels of discipline for various types of compliance violations. Perhaps you don't really know much about Human Resources operations or the laws governing that area. You go online, do some high-level research, and find a couple of apparently good sample sanctions policies, and you draft your policy. You think it's great and are relieved you can check it off your list as soon as your boss signs off on it.

When you meet with your boss, the CEO, who is busy and distracted, you explain that the policy is expected to be included in a compliance program and it sets the standards for how compliance violations are managed. The CEO asks whether the policy is typical for the industry, and you assert that it is and have found examples from other organizations. Your boss glances at the computer screen, the clock, and then signs off on it.

What just happened? You just jeopardized your relationship with Human Resources, for one thing. In addition, the policy may not be consistent with the company's progressive disciplinary policy. At some point, Human Resources will learn of the policy and will berate you for not knowing what you are doing and for doing it badly. You will have to redraft the policy, get an angry HR person to buy in to it (not easy, I promise), and then go back to your boss and explain what happened (unless, of course, someone has already complained about you and your boss knows of the problem). Now you have an enemy in HR, potentially, and your boss doesn't trust your judgment.

What should have happened in this example? You should have gotten to know the HR leader very early on. This person is on the Compliance Committee and can review the policies you draft. You should have first asked the HR leader for a meeting in which you are clear about what you need to do. You ask for help because this policy crosses into HR territory and you're not an HR expert. It's a very funny thing—when you tell people that they are the experts, not you, and that you need their help, they typically go out of their way to assist. If you come at them like you already know everything ... good luck getting any support. Especially if your knowledge isn't quite what you claim it is.

That's my general advice about policies: Make use of others' expertise, get them onboard, and be humble in the process. The only word of caution is to avoid giving the impression that you don't know anything. If stakeholders think you're incompetent, the strategy backfires. Do your homework before you talk to them, know their policies if possible, and understand generally what they do. Have outlines of what you need to accomplish, what other similar organizations do, and walk them through the information, asking for their guidance. Be organized and be respectful of their time. Common sense—but common sense isn't always common, as we all learn at some point.

Now, let's move on to some specific policies and standards you need in your compliance program.

# CODE OF CONDUCT

THE CODE OF CONDUCT (the Code) is the first document to develop, and is what the OIG is referencing when it includes "Standards of Conduct" as part of a compliance program requirement. Think of the compliance program as if you are building a house: The foundation has to be set before you worry about hanging gutters, right? The Code is your foundation, although it is not just a compliance document. The CEO or other key leader introduces the Code, and the document includes the organization's mission and values.

The Code lays out the compliance and ethics standards for the organization. Most codes of conduct include standards on patient rights, treatment of patients, and human resources–related topics such as equal employment opportunity and nondiscrimination. Environmental law and issues are often included, as are standards related to research conduct if the organization does research.

Privacy and security guidelines usually make up a significant section in the document, and an overview of policies on conflicts of interest, gifts, fraud, waste and abuse, and other compliance topics is included. Depending on the nature of the business, the Code may need to address specific risk areas, too.

The Code is a very important document, and it is one that the government expects to see. As you start assessing your organization and laying out the structure for the Code, bring many people into the process early. The first stop on your list should be HR, because not only is there a large HR component to the Code, but also an employee handbook might already contain some of the relevant material. At this point, you need to decide how much of it to include. Don't leave out critical issues such as nondiscrimination, but if the employee handbook is comprehensive, you can keep the Code high level on these topics and cross-reference the organization's employee handbook.

Keeping the Code as a big-picture view of the organization's standards and policies is a smart idea. If the underlying detailed policies change, you don't have to alter the Code document—which is a very good thing. Be sure to include the organization's policy position in the document, though, something to the effect of "Company X does not tolerate any form of discrimination based on sex, gender, age, national origin, race, or religion." That policy position won't change unless the laws add a new protected class, so putting it in the Code is another reminder to employees of what the company stands for.

This is another document for which a meeting with your pal in HR is important. Human Resources professionals understand a Code of Conduct and are generally supportive of creating that document if one doesn't already exist and of updating an existing document. Usually, HR is an ally on this project.

Information Security also needs to be involved as you develop the Code, because a large section should be devoted to the topic of information security and the organization's policies and procedures in that area. Identity theft and privacy breaches are significant risks in health care and can cause enormous harm to both patients and organizations. Policies and procedures vary to some degree across organizations and types of businesses, so this is one area where the expert really needs to own the section.

Another key element of the Code relates to fraud, waste, and abuse. The Code includes statements about accuracy of records and billing, and related items; but it should also include a section about the False Claims Act. As I mentioned earlier, the Deficit Reduction Act (DRA) requires organizations with $5 million or more in Medicaid revenue to include in their employee handbook information about the federal and state (if applicable) False Claims Acts, including information on how to be a whistleblower. I have found that, in organizations without a compliance program, or even without a well-experienced compliance officer, this piece may be missing. Some Human Resources people are not aware of this requirement, so it rarely shows up in an employee handbook. Many compliance officers manage this by putting it in the Code.

Answer two questions here: First, does your organization meet the threshold for having to include language on fraud, waste, and abuse? And second, is this subject already covered in the employee handbook? Don't be surprised if few or none in your organization knows about the DRA. It was passed in 2006 and caused a flurry for a year or so, but it doesn't seem to come up much anymore, especially with people outside of the compliance arena. Telling employees how to blow the whistle is also highly unpopular in organizations. Legal doesn't like it (although members of that department should be aware of it, unless they are new and haven't worked in health care long), and Finance certainly doesn't appreciate it, either. So, when you take your first draft to the Compliance Committee, make sure you've reviewed the DRA. Maybe even print out an article for them about what you need to do; resources abound online.

The Code of Conduct is an area where you want to have established good relations with other functional areas in advance. Depending on the size of the organization and its politics, you might solicit input from a number of people on the front end. This reduces your risk of getting beat up later. It may seem obvious, but make sure the Legal department reviews the document. Any attorneys on the Compliance Committee should see the draft of the Code in advance of the committee meeting. The last thing you want is to get everyone else to approve the document and then find out that Legal has yet to review it … and the lawyers have a number of changes to make. This is how never-ending review cycles begin, and it's how you end up with multiple "final" documents.

Ask for input from your CEO on the approval process for this document because it does affect the whole company. Who needs to approve this document? The Code may go from the Compliance Committee to an executive committee, then perhaps to an executive medical committee. The board should approve the Code—the document is that important.

You need to be comfortable explaining why the company needs a Code of Conduct, or why the two-page policy called the Code of Conduct that was written ten years ago and never revised isn't adequate. The easy answer is to whip out the OIG guidance and read aloud the section on policies and standards. But beyond that, leaders should understand that the Code really demonstrates to employees the value the organization places on ethical behavior in the workplace and how people should treat each other.

Publishing the Code in a nice glossy booklet shows an investment by leadership, much more so than housing an outdated policy in a three-ring binder that gathers dust on the shelf. If your organization is merging with another or is making organization-level changes, the Code is a nice piece of branding that shows that all divisions and locations are part of the same organization. That aspect can appeal to leadership. Last, the Code should include an acknowledgment page that employees sign, indicating that they have received and will comply with the Code. The signature page can come in handy during discipline issues when an employee has violated the Code. Human Resources and Legal, in particular, like this feature.

Although much of this sounds rather simple to enact (of course we don't discriminate or submit false claims, right?), it is not easy at all. Fights will erupt over sections of this document on topics like conflicts of interest and gifts. I have even been attacked in a board meeting over the institution of an anonymous hotline (I explain why and how to set up a hotline later). You just never know which parts of the policy will cause issues, but it is quite likely that they will. Just when you want to complete the Code and move on to getting other policies in place, you will probably get mired in some of these issues while trying to ascertain what the specific standards should be. If you haven't been through a gifts or conflicts-of-interest debate with healthcare leaders, you may be in for an experience.

The good news is that you will have the organization's overarching policy positions ironed out by the time you get through the Code. The bad news is that you will feel like you are falling behind where you wanted to be in terms of time and accomplishments. In larger organizations, be very conservative in work planning when it comes to the Code and key policies. I have seen a Code get approved within a couple of weeks of being drafted; I have also seen a mere revision take a year or two. I'm just warning you so you can plan accordingly.

If your organization doesn't have a Code of Conduct, a good strategy is to find a nice model to show the CEO. Tell him or her that the Code is one of the first policies you must write, and solicit thoughts on how challenging it might be to gain buy-in and approval. If you're new to the company, such a discussion could prove quite useful, and it will also improve the CEO's understanding of what you are doing and why.

# POLICIES

Let's talk now about drafting policies. First, I would like to introduce some basic issues you might encounter.

When you start in an organization as a new compliance officer, policy creation will be a key part of your job, especially at first. There is a natural order to the compliance process:

1. You complete an assessment to identify compliance risks in the compliance program or in the organization in general.
2. You do necessary research and then draft policies using key stakeholders as a resource.
3. You train employees and leadership on those policies.

4. You institute a monitoring and auditing process to verify that the policies are being followed.

5. You create corrective action plans when you find deficiencies, and factor those issues into your annual risk assessment.

When you consider the order of this process, you can see that drafting policies is the priority after program structure and Code of Conduct are established.

The words *policies, standards,* and *guidelines* mean different things in different organizations. You may be surprised at how passionately people can fight over the definitions and distinctions. Just to be perfectly clear, *policies* are documents outlining requirements that must be met. *Guidelines* typically describe preferred processes or activities that the organization recommends. *Standards,* more regulatory sounding, usually are understood to be requirements as well. Look to your organization's webpage or other location where such documents may be housed, and maybe talk to a couple of people about how the organization distinguishes among policies, standards, and guidelines if it isn't clear, just so you approach the issue in a way that employees will understand. Compliance policies are *not* guidelines.

As you orient to your new role, stakeholders may tell you about various policies that they believe are needed (and that you need to draft!). Or, as you review the existing policies, you might see gaps. At this point, get ahold of the organization's policy template to work off of so that you don't have to reformat the policies later. Small organizations may not actually have a template; in large organizations, likely someone owns the template and is very particular about its usage. If that is the case, befriend this person, because getting your policies posted will be much easier when that person is happy to help.

If no template exists, you can develop one. Make sure the template is structured in a way that the policy makes sense to anyone who reads it (in other words, not just the lawyers!) and that the purpose of the policy is understandable.

I'm sure some people believe there is only one correct way to draft a policy; of course, I have my own opinion, based on experience. In reality, policy creation varies by organization. A very small healthcare practice is a simple organization, and you can include procedures in policies if you choose. For large organizations, or geographically diverse companies, it makes more sense to include in policies high-level procedural requirements, not details on how to implement the requirements, because different locations will have different processes, and you will get a lot of resistance from the people who can't implement the policy the way the procedures are specifically outlined in the document. If you have business in multiple states, relevant state laws can be another wrinkle that should encourage you to consider allowing policies to cover the bigger picture.

Start your policy with a section titled "PURPOSE." This statement tells the reader why the policy must be followed and why it was created in the first place. A purpose statement for a policy on fraud and abuse might read something like this: "The purpose of this policy is to provide all employees, contractors, students, and other agents of Company X with standards and guidance for preventing fraud, waste, and abuse in the organization." Or an alternative: "The purpose of this policy is to comply with the state and federal False Claims Act, Anti-Kickback Statute, the Stark Law, and any other applicable fraud, waste, and abuse laws and regulations." The second example is obviously more formal and might have been written by an attorney.

Base your choice of tone on how other policies are worded if you have a formalized policy structure. If you don't, then you can decide the best tone for policies in your organization. One caveat: Even if previous policies merely copy regulatory language, don't follow that lead. It's time to move the organization toward policies that employees can actually understand and follow.

I often see policies that include the heading "POLICY," and then the rest of the document contains a list of statements or regulatory language. That's not really the best way to present policies to the organization, in my view. But, I admit, I am a policy geek and have definite opinions on these things.

The policy statement should be just that:

> It is the policy of Company X to comply with all state and federal laws, rules, and regulations that address fraud, waste, and abuse and to ensure that all employees are provided training on the laws and policies relating to fraud and abuse that pertain to their jobs.

I'm not holding this out as *the* policy statement you should use, but you get the idea. I like to have a sentence that follows to clarify what the rest of the document includes and to whom it applies:

> It is the expectation of Company X that employees, agents, and students whose roles are impacted by this policy adhere to the procedures outlined below.

This statement makes it clear that any procedural requirements are part of the policy itself and are not optional.

Another key section sometimes needed is "DEFINITIONS." For instance, in a non-retaliation policy, I think it is absolutely necessary to define the term *retaliation*. Otherwise, if employees violate the policy, they can claim they didn't realize that what they did was retaliation. For instance:

> Retaliation: Any adverse employment action that is taken against an employee as a result of that employee engaging in good faith reporting or cooperating in a legitimate investigation.

For this section, it is useful also to provide examples, either in conjunction with the definition or in a section on procedures.

A section titled "BACKGROUND" can be useful, though I don't think you have to include definitions or background in every policy. No need to put unnecessary words on paper. A background section can set the policy in context. For instance,

> Retaliation is prohibited under many laws, such as the federal False Claims Act, which states that an organization may not retaliate against an individual who is making a good faith report under the requirements of that law. … Retaliation is also not allowed for good faith reporting of concerns under Title VII for Equal Employment. … Employees reporting concerns under these statutes are considered "protected" with respect to reporting or cooperating with investigations related to those issues.

In other words, the background explains where the policy stems from and supplies the reason why employees need to take it seriously. I think that including this piece, where it's relevant, gives the policy teeth and puts employees on notice that this is a serious issue, that legal reasons for the policy exist, and that violations will be handled accordingly. You can also address contextual information like this in the Purpose section; you can decide which makes more sense. The main idea is to avoid redundancies that might creep in for the sake of having consistent sections in all policies. Policies should individually include all relevant information, but should not be repetitive or difficult to comprehend.

Some policies have a section called "SCOPE." This isn't a bad idea, although not required if you craft your policy statement in a way that includes scope. But it doesn't hurt to make it clear:

> This policy applies to all employees, contractors, temporary employees, students, residents, volunteers, medical staff, and board members.

Be careful, by the way, before you include medical staff in the scope. Make sure the medical staff bylaws don't conflict with the policy. For example, if the medical staff bylaws state that medical staff must comply with all hospital policies, you're fine. I recommend checking on this issue early on, and it's certainly in your best interest to have some physicians on your side! Getting medical staff bylaws changed, especially by the Compliance department, is a process not likely to be completed without a great degree of pain and suffering—if at all—so be aware.

The section "PROCEDURES" is important, and most policies should have one. Include only what I call "core standards" in the Procedures section. For instance, if the policy is about excluded provider checking, don't proscribe whose role it is to conduct the check (because this might change and you would have to amend the policy wording), but rather which types of people need to be checked and how often (information unlikely to change). Also state that documentation must be maintained to demonstrate such checks have been completed. Some companies outsource this task, so the policy need not state *how* documentation gets done.

I have heard many arguments about policies versus procedures, and my position is this: The policy states what needs to be done and the minimum core standards that meet the policy's requirements. The individuals or departments whose jobs are affected need to write their own procedures, because they are in the best position to determine how to comply. Compliance may, however, do a review at any time to validate that the policy requirements are being met, or may review the procedures themselves for the same reason. Once I explain to employees that my job is to set standards to keep us in compliance, not to manage their operations, they are much more amenable. As soon as people understand that, they are also more likely to ask you to weigh in on their procedures to make sure they meet the policy requirements.

Another section I like to see in policies is "RELATED POLICIES AND PROCEDURES." This is typically a list of policies and procedures that either relate to or are affected by the policy at hand. This makes it easier for employees to know which other documents are available. Although the information may be readily available on the policy list online, this section is helpful for readers of the paper document and when the policy list is long, which makes it difficult to identify related documents. It also helps employees locate policies that may have unexpected titles. You may be surprised at some of the policies titles that exist in your organization, making it difficult for employees to find simply by searching.

Also, policies should always include an effective date and revision dates. Each document should show its revision date. This is essential for purposes of version control and can become relevant if your organization is ever under investigation. You need to be able to show which policies were in effect at the time of any incident.

Last, depending on the size of the organization, it is important to know which policies are already in place. You can avoid big trouble later by making sure the Code of Conduct or policies you draft do not contradict existing policies or practices. Policies are usually kept on company intranet sites, linked at the corporate level as well as by department. The organization's internal website is a good place to search, but know that not all departments diligently publish their policies online or update them there. Some organizations do not even have an intranet site. Spending a little time on the front end to conduct this inventory will save you potential grief in the long run.

So, let's get into the actual policies now.

### *Non-Retaliation*

Non-retaliation was discussed briefly earlier. A non-retaliation policy is expected to be included in a compliance program. Frequently, similar policies related to non-retaliation for sexual harassment or discrimination claims are housed in the Human Resources department. For that reason you may even be told that you don't need to create a non-retaliation policy. I have always stood my ground about needing this particular document, but there is nothing wrong with working with Human Resources to modify its policies and broaden them to include comprehensive coverage of non-retaliation for employee compliance reporting or cooperation with a compliance investigation.

There are several key items to include in this document. First, include a policy statement that clearly explains that the organization has a non-retaliation policy and that retaliation will not be tolerated. Second, include the definition of non-retaliation, which is particularly important for this policy for the reasons I stated earlier. You don't want a manager who retaliates against an employee to be able to claim he or she did not consider the behavior in question to constitute retaliation.

*Retaliation* is any adverse employment-related action taken against an employee in response to that employee's good faith reporting or cooperation with a legitimate investigation. Adverse employment-related actions comprise many practices, not just termination. Many cases of retaliation involve removing an employee from situations in which the employee has the opportunity to report or to interact with others. Employees may have their duties changed, may be excluded from meetings, or may have their desk or office moved to a more remote location. These steps are taken to put employees in a box and make it more difficult for them to discuss their concerns.

One obvious form of retaliation includes suddenly negative performance evaluations for employees who have a good record and whom other employees believe are good and responsible employees. Another common form of retaliation is termination or even a leave of absence given for a questionable reason.

Another important element of this policy—and of all your policies—is a statement that describes how noncompliance with the policy will lead to disciplinary action, up to and including termination. It is *not* correct to state that violating the policy can lead to fines or jail time. Erroneous statements like this are frequently included in policies based on fraud and abuse or other laws. However, it is not the violation of the policy that can land an employee in jail, but the violation of the underlying law that will lead to trouble with law enforcement. The organization does not have the authority to send an employee to jail, of course, so be aware of this wording issue when crafting this section of the compliance policy. It is correct to describe the disciplinary action that will result from violating the policy and then to include a separate explanation of the potential consequences for violating the underlying laws or regulations; just be clear about the distinction.

When you roll out this policy, discuss it widely to promote understanding among organizational leaders, managers, Human Resources staff, and employees. Although everyone will say that retaliation is not tolerated, retaliation often is an insidious problem that leaders are unaware of. Part of the problem is managers' lack of understanding of what constitutes retaliation, and sometimes even Human Resources will align with management in taking corrective action that borders on or amounts to retaliation.

One example has to do with anonymous reporting. The first thing managers often do when they hear an anonymous complaint has been made about their department is to try to figure out who complained.

Sometimes they have a very good idea who reported. They have a tendency to go straight to that employee to try to talk about the issue. At that point you need to remind managers about the non-retaliation policy. It can be very difficult to prevent managers from approaching employees, even if their intentions are not negative but rather to understand or clear up a misconception. When employees want to remain anonymous, they often have a reason to do so, or at least they believe that they do. If a manager approaches an employee who is trying to remain anonymous, the employee will lose trust in the reporting process and will likely tell coworkers that reporting doesn't work and advise them not to report because there is no anonymity or protection.

Talk to some employees privately (or use a survey) and ask them how they feel about the hotline that is available for anonymous reporting, about reporting compliance concerns, and about how much they trust the process. You will quickly learn whether the organization's employees perceive management, Human Resources, or even Compliance as trustworthy. You may be surprised how many organizations suffer from this feeling among employees. It's important to know whether you are dealing with this lack of trust and to identify its cause. I have seen trust problems develop from a single incident that was handled badly when the harmed employee subsequently told coworkers the details. Those sorts of stories spread like wildfire and can make your job a lot more difficult.

Another point to emphasize with managers is that they need to pay attention to employees who raise concerns or "complain." It is a good idea when educating managers to remind them that employees who are perceived as complainers or troublemakers may be raising legitimate concerns that must be considered. When managers think an employee is just trying to cause trouble, they are more likely to handle that employee badly, which then can degenerate into a claim of retaliation.

Also remind managers how whistleblowers are created: If an employee is ignored or retaliated against, and that employee believes a concern is legitimate, he or she may pursue it outside of the organization. This is an important point to make in training on the non-retaliation policy. People need to fully understand what retaliation is and how it can manifest in the organization. Then they need to be reminded how government investigations are triggered: most often by a whistleblower who was not handled properly by the employer.

Although the non-retaliation policy should be relatively straightforward, be sure to ask Human Resources to review it before you take it to the Compliance Committee.

### *False Claims Act/Fraud and Abuse*

One critical policy to include is the fraud and abuse policy. Some organizations have a False Claims Act policy, which can be traced back to the Deficit Reduction Act and the requirements in that law relating to both state and federal False Claims Act education. Given that financial arrangements, which often implicate the Stark Law and the Anti-Kickback Statute, are a significant source of whistleblower cases and government investigations, I think it is an excellent idea to create a broad fraud and abuse policy that covers the state and federal False Claims Act, the Stark Law, and the Anti-Kickback Statute.

The policy needs to state that the organization will comply with all applicable fraud and abuse laws, including but not limited to the state and federal False Claims Act, the Stark Law, and the Anti-Kickback Statute. If other significant laws apply to your organization and fit in with the fraud and abuse policy, certainly list those as well.

For this policy, probably the best way to cover the requirements under each law is by including a background section in which you explain each law clearly and thoroughly and in a way that is as readable as possible for a typical employee. In other words, cutting and pasting the regulatory and legal language is not the best way to handle this. If you don't have a strong understanding of these laws, get the Legal department to help. You will want Legal to review this policy anyhow.

Because fraud and abuse laws can be violated in a variety of ways, writing comprehensive procedures is difficult unless you create a many-paged policy (which isn't the best way to go). I recommend including core procedural requirements that relate to the various laws. For instance, many of the issues covered in Stark and Anti-Kickback relate to financial arrangements and contracts. A core procedure in the fraud and abuse policy that addresses the requirements of this legislation requires a robust contract approval process in place in the organization, a process that includes review by Legal of any financial arrangements involving physicians and other referral sources.

The core procedure would also include a statement that the organization has set procedures that ensure lease arrangements and other arrangements with referral sources are for fair market value, are commercially reasonable, and are not related to volume or value of referrals. Look for examples online, review the laws as well as OIG guidance to identify key risk issues for your line of business, and create high-level procedural requirements to address those.

Another significant area to cover in the fraud and abuse policy relates to claims accuracy, appropriate coding and billing, and medical necessity. The submission of inaccurate claims to government programs has been a core compliance issue since the beginning of compliance programs, and it is still the "bread and butter" of compliance. Do your homework on your organization's lines of business to identify specific regulations, risk areas, and enforcement trends that could affect the company, and then create procedures accordingly.

For a fraud and abuse policy to be effective, it takes a lot of work and help from stakeholders. Think about the procedures you are writing and who will need to review or create procedures to comply with the fraud and abuse procedural requirements. Most likely, these stakeholders are Legal, Contracting, Purchasing, Medical Affairs, Marketing, and Coding and Billing management, at a minimum. You want Finance on your side as well. All of these people need to be involved with policy development before you take a draft of the policy to the Compliance Committee.

I believe this policy should ultimately be approved by the board or board committee. It's a very important policy; it makes a good statement to have it approved by the board and, doubly, you have an opportunity to educate the board or Committee on fraud and abuse in the context of presenting this policy.

Something else to consider is that fraud and abuse may be addressed in multiple places within the organization, including in the Code of Conduct, perhaps in the employee handbook, as well as in department or division-level policies. You need to identify those documents and make sure they are all consistent, which can be a challenge in a large organization. Any conflicts in procedures should come up during the vetting process, however, so synchronization most likely will happen during policy development if you have identified all key stakeholders. This is just an issue to be aware of.

Educating staff, management, leaders, board members, medical staff, and other consultants, residents, and so forth is necessary, and it needs to be documented. Fraud and abuse education should be included in new employee orientation and annual education. Additional education, with emphasis on the applicable procedures, should be developed for key risk areas. When you identify your risk areas, think broadly. Who receives donations for medical staff education? Who goes out and markets to physicians and other referral sources? Which departments enter into contracts? You may have a separate department, for instance, that manages leases.

Back in the old days, we thought of the coders and billers as our high-risk area. Although coding and billing will always be an area with risk, the largest settlements and repayments these days frequently relate to kickbacks and medical necessity. Privacy and security violations are also starting to get expensive. The point here is that areas constituting high risk have evolved and increased, so you need to really learn your organization and the functions of all departments, and then target specific procedures to mitigate the risks.

### *Conflicts of Interest*

The conflicts of interest policy actually is a policy and a procedure. A staple of any compliance program, it describes a disclosure process that individuals in certain roles use to disclose any potential conflicts of interest. A *conflict of interest* is any situation in which an individual's interests may be at odds with the interests of the organization.

Typically, conflicts of interest are financial, such as an ownership interest in a competitor or a vendor, participation on the board of a competitor or a vendor, or a material financial arrangement between the employee and a competitor or a vendor. Another potential conflict is when employees own their own business whose activities somehow conflict with the company's, or when employees use the company to further their own business.

For example, an employee tries to sell his or her company's products or services to other employees or, even worse, to patients. Some conflicts of interest involve time commitments; these are typically referred to as conflicts of commitment. For instance, an individual works for a healthcare company but consults on the side, and the consulting job cuts into the time the employee works for the organization.

The conflict of interest policy applies to all employees, board members, consultants, and medical staff. Although the disclosure process does not include all individuals, it is important to understand that all employees need to disclose conflicts and should avoid conflict situations. Consider the employee with his or her own business as a good example. A nursing assistant may run an assisted living facility out of her home and recruit residents from the facility where she is employed. This employee would not typically be subject to the disclosure requirement (as explained below) but should disclose this situation voluntarily, because it does suggest a conflict of interest and could potentially affect performance.

The disclosure process applies to anyone in management who has hiring, purchasing, or contracting authority; medical staff; and board members. Some organizations also create a disclosure process for committees that make purchasing decisions or decisions about hiring vendors. If that type of committee operates in your organization, a best practice is to have members conduct a committee disclosure process at the beginning of any project.

There are some important operational points to share about this process. First, the disclosure process should occur at hiring and annually thereafter for affected individuals. In addition, if an employee moves from a nondisclosure position to a role that requires disclosure, a complete disclosure should be made as part of the job change.

Another item to consider is who reviews the disclosures, and how any potential conflicts will be managed. Typically, the compliance officer manages the conflict of interest annual process and collects disclosures.

Most disclosures are not problematic; frequently, they involve trivial situations like a spouse working at another healthcare organization, but not in a role that affects your organization. Stock ownership is another common disclosure.

You should create an escalation process, however, for any disclosure that is not simple to resolve or, I would add, that can potentially be political, needing special handling. Part of your success as a compliance officer depends on your ability to discern situations that could blow up and to make sure you get the necessary assistance in managing them to avoid as much drama as possible. The chief executive most commonly will be your sounding board, but it might also be another objective person, such as legal counsel or someone from Human Resources. Discuss the escalation process with the Compliance Committee, because these questions will arise when you launch the disclosure process.

It is important to help people understand that a disclosure is not necessarily a bad thing; it just means that the issue needs to be reviewed and a possible mitigation strategy put in place. Perhaps, for instance, an individual is removed from a decision-making role relating to a vendor with whom the employee has an interest. We talk more about these processes in the vendors section in Part II.

There are different ways to implement and track the disclosure process, such as with electronic tools.

For larger organizations, electronic tools present the easiest approach, because they enable you to distribute and track disclosure forms, make reporting much easier, and identify who has not responded so you can pursue those disclosures. And be prepared for the chase—it will happen, so allow plenty of time for that part of the process.

Electronic systems might not make as much sense for smaller organizations. Instead, you can create a tracking spreadsheet that lists all the affected persons. Be sure, however, that you get a current list from all categories of employees, medical staff, and other agents, including people in consulting roles, medical directors, and others who might not be in the Human Resources or medical staff database. Obtaining an accurate list can be challenging, depending on the organization; so again, be prepared and be grateful when these processes move smoothly.

One area that can be problematic is disclosures about gifts. Gifts are always a difficult topic in organizations that allow them. Gifts can be not only a violation of policy, but also problematic with respect to the Anti-Kickback Statute and the Stark Law, depending on who gives the gift and who receives it.

It is not far-fetched for a gift to violate the Anti-Kickback Statute, and under that statute the giver and receiver can be liable. A violation can be found if "one purpose" of the gift is related to getting referrals for services that are reimbursed under government healthcare programs. If the gift is to a physician, Stark may be an issue—again, depending on the facts—and with Stark, there is no requirement for intent; it is a strict liability statute.

I mention all this because you need to understand the importance of the conflict of interest policy and the nexus of gifts, conflicts of interest, and violations of law. You will be presented many questions in this area, and some of them will be tricky to resolve. It is important you understand the laws and policies that apply, as well as the operational realities. It is vital to ensure that your conflicts of interest policy, gifts policy, and Code of Conduct align, as well as any other departmental policies. Areas with related policies might include medical staff and purchasing. Work with the Compliance Committee on how to address the issue of gifts disclosure.

And remember, a potential conflict of interest is not necessarily a bad thing; it's just an issue that needs to be handled appropriately and documented. It is also important to make sure your leadership's view is consistent with the policies and your decision making, because this is such a volatile area, one that can get people agitated. People do not like the implication that their judgment is impaired by a meal or token gift, so keep that in mind when you have to deal with their reactions to potential conflicts of interest.

### *Gifts*

It makes sense to follow the Conflicts of Interest section of this book with one on gifts. The gifts policy is an expected part of a compliance program; it can be covered in the Conflicts of Interest or Vendor Relations policies, or may be a stand-alone document. Before you even begin drafting this policy, pull and review some resources. First, have a general understanding of the Stark and Anti-Kickback laws, as referenced above. Also, the Pharmaceutical Research and Manufacturers of America (PhRMA) and the Advanced Medical Technology Association (AdvaMed) publish industry guidelines for pharmacy and device manufacturers. These documents are available online and provide guidance to their respective industries, including standards relating to the practice of giving gifts and other perks. You need to be as well informed as possible, both about these legal and quasi-regulatory documents and policies of other similar organizations.

Depending on the organization, gifts might be your biggest challenge. Although the PhRMA and AdvaMed guidance documents have been out for many years, and many huge government settlements have included kickbacks as part of the case, some organizations continue the practice of courting or being courted with "boondoggle" trips and tickets to sporting and golfing events, to name a few.

You will know early on when you work on the Code of Conduct with the Compliance Committee exactly what type of organization yours is. Many healthcare companies aligned with the conservative side of this issue early on and banned all gifts and meals, period. One practical reason is that they don't want to have to keep track of gifts—and if the organization allows gifts, they should be tracked. This is particularly important if your organization gives gifts to physicians. Under Stark, these "incidental benefits" are limited to $392 a year (the amount is adjusted from time to time, so you will need to update your policy if you specify the dollar amount).

So, what is the correct standard? It depends on who you ask. Rather than push forward with your opinion, find out what the current culture and practice are. If you have landed in an organizational culture where giving and receiving pricey gifts is the norm, you have much more work to do than you would in a conservative organization. I prefer no gifts at all—it's just easier and cleaner—but some organizations will never adopt this policy. If that is the case, pinpoint the most problematic types of gifts from a legal perspective and start there.

Gifts to physicians and referral sources and gifts from vendors present the biggest risks. Executives receiving goodies from business associates, for instance, from an insurance broker, is not as risky as can be physicians receiving gifts from a hospital. I don't like these gifts to leaders and continually remind leadership such gift exchanges give an appearance of impropriety and do not demonstrate the mission to employees … you may not get traction with such arguments. If anyone demands to know the legal risk, you know you are going to have a problem, because the issue is not that black and white with respect to gifts for the C-Suite. Pick your battles.

If you do allow gifts, certain core standards apply. First, meals given as gifts must be "modest," and you will need to repeat this often. Trying to put a dollar limit on "modest" is not easy, though. I have found that dollar thresholds in general are challenging, although sometimes necessary. Meals, if you allow them, should be provided only in conjunction with legitimate business or educational sessions. Second, vendors should not pay for the organization's employees' travel expenses unless that is part of a contractual arrangement, such as when vendors sponsor annual product information demonstrations on-site, or something like that. It is far preferable to incorporate such arrangements into written agreements. We talk in more depth about purchasing and vendors later.

Language that should become second nature to you when drafting documents related to gifts or financial arrangements with referral sources has to do with referrals themselves. In every appropriate place, such as in the Code of Conduct, in policies, in the employee handbook, and certainly in contracts, include language to the effect that the organization "does not offer, give, or accept any gifts, benefits, discounts, or other remuneration in exchange for referrals."

Why else would a vendor offer gifts except in exchange for business? Both parties of a kickback transaction may be found culpable, and if "one purpose" of the activity is to gain referrals ... well, there you go. The OIG worries not only about costs to government programs, but also about the influence of such gifts on decision making and the impact on patient care. These suggestions outrage physicians—and I don't blame them, really—but studies show that even a small gift affects prescribing habits. It's not conscious: Physicians can't be "bought" with a pen. But the quid pro quo effect exists nonetheless.

One recent development related to the issue of gifts is the Open Payments database, which came about as a result of the Physician Payments Sunshine Act of 2010. In sum, this law requires pharmaceutical and device manufacturers to report all gifts given to physicians and teaching hospitals. Physicians and affected hospitals that have registered with the database have an opportunity to review the disclosures in advance of publication within a certain time frame. It is a good idea to make sure physicians in your organization know about the Open Payments database, and it's important you are aware of it, too, because you can check up on disclosures and activities using this database.

The gift policy applies to all employees, contractors, medical staff, residents, and others (students, volunteers, etc.). Be sure to include the key provisions in new employee orientation material, as well as in annual compliance education sessions. I have found that the topics that garner the most questions asked during in-person education are gifts and privacy. I address privacy subsequently.

### *Contract Management*

Contract management in not always considered a compliance policy. If it's not, I recommend that you make sure it exists somewhere in the organization. A contract management policy and procedure are necessary because, of all the risk areas in health care, the largest settlements result from faulty financial arrangements. If you don't have controls in place around the contracting process, the risk can be astronomical. In addition, when it comes to arrangements with physicians, if the organization pays them, you need to be able to show the specific agreements that describe the arrangements. Although the Stark rules have eased a bit, you still need a contract; it's too soon to say how the loosened provisions will be enforced.

You might find a contracting authority matrix in place. This document delineates who can authorize and sign contracts. Small practices and organizations usually don't have a matrix, because typically the CEO signs contracts. Larger organizations, however, need a matrix to establish the level of management or leader who has authority to approve agreements. The CEO, for instance, has greater approval power than a vice-president. So, when you start looking into the issue of contract management, find the contract authority matrix first. Start by asking Finance; frequently, this department owns the document. (One interesting issue to watch for during the exploration stage is whether the organization in actuality allows people to sign contracts who aren't authorized to.)

With the matrix document in hand and an understanding of how contract approval is carried out in the culture, you can write the contract management policy. Because different departments may have different procedures, either segment the policy or keep it high level, by simply stating that a contract approval process is in place for any purchasing or contracting function that operates in accordance with the contract approval matrix, and so on. The contract management policy applies to all management personnel and leadership who have contracting or purchasing authority and who have a role in managing contracts.

The main point is to ensure that an objective and structured process is in place, and that you review it and believe that it meets the objectivity standard. The policy should also state that any individual with a personal or financial interest in the subject of the contract is barred from approving the agreement and that an objective alternative will be identified. You can set this up however it best fits your organizational structure, but the policy and core procedures should be in place.

Physician arrangements must be approved by legal counsel. In the contract management policy, include the recommended language about referrals: that no physician arrangements are entered for the purpose of obtaining referrals and that the organization doesn't calculate compensation based on the volume or value of referrals. Drill this into everyone like a mantra because, from a business perspective, it is natural for the organization to consider the business benefits of certain arrangements, and this tendency can be hard to overcome.

But this is no man's land—it can't be overstated. No discussion, no minutes, no contracts should even suggest an organization has such a motivation as it relates to compensation. After all, if the organization gets into trouble, all written notes, policies, and documents are subject to discovery; and you don't want to have to explain away meeting minutes that document the executive team discussing the number of patients a specific physician would bring in if hired. Those sorts of discussions cannot happen, and part of your job is to help leadership understand that by baking it in to the organizational culture. It's also a good idea to make sure administrative staff, who take minutes, understand these issues as well, since you won't be in every meeting. This can also help keep those discussions and documentation to a minimum.

After the approval process is set, create a process for monitoring arrangements to ensure that renewals are handled in a timely manner and that related documents, such as licensure and insurance, are kept current. For large organizations, there are software vendors that can help with this step; but, again, in a small practice or company, that's overkill and not the best use of resources. Mainly, make sure your system tracks the contract owner, approver, and any updates or renewals that are needed. Keep in mind, again, to allow yourself plenty of time to manage physician arrangements, because changes or negotiation may be involved.

It's essential renewals are kept up-to-date, especially for physician arrangements. Even if your organization has a propensity for evergreen contracts, which renew automatically, someone must review those arrangements, as well. Without a process ensuring that all agreements are reviewed routinely, you may end up with an agreement that is no longer needed or for terms that are no longer acceptable. In one organization, a vendor was being paid a huge sum for a system that had never been implemented or used. Those kinds of examples are useful for persuading leaders of the essential need to closely monitor all arrangements.

### *Record Retention*

I admit, record retention is not exciting, but it is an expected component of a compliance program. A few points about record retention bear mentioning. First, record retention does not apply only to clinical records. When you think of how records can come into play, for instance, in a lawsuit or a government action, much more than clinical service records will be required. Each department in your organization—Human Resources, Finance, Administration, Internal Audit, Compliance, Legal—generates relevant records that must be retained. On the clinical side, more than just charts need to be maintained; X-rays, nursing training, medical staff bylaws, provider credentialing, and even emails must be managed. You see where I am going with this. All of these records must have identified periods of retention and, yes, destruction.

Second, a record retention policy is also a record destruction policy. Destruction is a step often overlooked in records management policies. In the policy that addresses record destruction, state that records are destroyed in accordance with the time frames delineated in the record retention schedule. In addition, the method for destruction is well documented and consistent. Keep a written record of how the records were destroyed (shredding, incineration, etc.), who completed the destruction, and the date. In litigation or a government investigation, these records (of your record management and destruction) are essential for demonstrating that your company did not "shred the evidence" in anticipation of a pending legal matter.

What you want to prevent is various departments handling destruction however they see fit, and at their convenience. This is a most typical situation, unless an organization has hired a record storage company, which understands the importance of proper destruction. Records must be kept and destroyed on a regular schedule. In a potential lawsuit, you can imagine how hard inconsistent record retention is to justify to opposing counsel. Can you picture having to explain that the department had a system upgrade and was very, very busy and didn't get around to purging records for two years because they were buried? No, that's not a good position to be in.

A sticky area has to do with electronic medical records (EMRs). It's easy to identify the date a paper record was created, and then to subject it to the record retention process. The question I am often asked is whether an organization must purge EMRs when it is infeasible to sort them by date. These, and other issues, are evolving as health care transitions from paper to electronic records. There are a number of unanswered questions because this is a new set of issues. For now,

I advise you to treat all records the same. If that is not an option, then document the process you do use and make sure it's followed consistently. Ideally, the vendors that create the electronic medical records systems will become aware of this issue and fix their systems accordingly.

The standard for retention is to follow state or federal laws, whichever are stricter. State laws vary, and at this point, so do Medicare laws, with managed care plans subject to longer retention periods than traditional Medicare records. In many cases, no laws govern the retention of various obscure records, such as maintenance logs for various pieces of equipment. In such instances, investigate whether an industry standard exists, talk to people in the department affected, and if you still find no answers, resort to civil laws. Typically, if you retain records for seven years past year end, you are covered for civil cases. But you need to check all this out—this is not legal advice! Your Legal department or counsel should weigh in on these sorts of questions before you finalize a record retention policy and schedule, because this is fundamentally a legal issue that can have far-reaching consequences if handled incorrectly. Lastly, make sure that your record retention policy addresses the issue of 'legal holds', which occur when records need to be retained due to litigation. Discuss this matter with legal counsel to make sure it's covered appropriately.

### *Auditing and Monitoring*

Auditing and monitoring are parts of a compliance program, and as such require a policy. This area may be broader than you originally anticipate, however. The traditional thinking is based on auditing and monitoring of coding and billing, but that is only the beginning. Your policies and processes need to address the entire compliance program, so think about all the issues and risk areas mentioned so far. They, and others discussed in this book, should be monitored, at a minimum.

What is the difference between auditing and monitoring? Auditing is performed by an objective person or group that is not part of the department and that may, in fact, not even be internal to the organization. Think of Internal Audit, Compliance, and outside consultants. Auditing is a formal process that evaluates the existing processes and controls and verifies that they are working correctly. Audits usually are reported, perhaps to the Compliance Committee, to executive management, or to the board.

Monitoring, on the other hand, is a routine part of operations. The operational owner runs reports, checks for outliers, explores denials, and uncovers other issues to verify whether processes are working according to the existing policies, procedures, and requirements. Monitoring is typically internal to the department or function and may or may not be reported to the compliance officer.

So, what should be monitored? What about hiring or contracting with excluded providers? Yes, you need to be on top of that, and documentation needs to be maintained to show that checks are conducted. What about financial arrangements, especially with physicians? Absolutely. And gifts? Oh, yes, gifts. And when you think about coding and billing, consider the new world we live in: not your old-school coding and billing world. Now we must keep tabs on data related to quality indicators, readmissions, hospital-acquired conditions, and medical necessity … so much needs to be monitored or audited. Coding and billing do still matter, of course, both in terms of ongoing monitoring and more formal auditing.

You can use a variety of ways to keep on top of these areas without having to do the work yourself. The departments responsible for these functions usually have processes in place to identify trends and problems. If they don't, your work is cut out for you. Assuming monitoring processes are set up, you need to work with the departments to get in the loop on their reviews. Find out about their processes related to coding and documentation: How do they check on the adequacy of physician documentation? How do they validate that coding is accurate? What is the process for reviewing the work of coders? In terms of billing, what quality control processes exist? And who is keeping track of denials and following up?

Find out what the feedback loop is from billing, coding, and documentation reviews. Your organization might institute a Revenue Cycle or Revenue Integrity Committee that includes these functions and meets to work through identified issues. If there is such a group, the compliance officer needs to be part of it. If there is not such a group, perhaps you can encourage one to form, unless another adequate mechanism for coordination is available.

The compliance auditing and monitoring policy does not need to be highly detailed about the types of audits conducted, so long as you have documented processes in place for auditing and monitoring identified risk areas. Be sure to include a statement outlining how audits are identified and managed, both planned or routine audits and "risk-based" audits. The auditing and monitoring policy should discuss the creation of an annual compliance work plan, which includes audits, and how those work plan audits are identified.

You can create a separate policy for compliance risk assessments. It also makes sense simply to include in the auditing and monitoring policy discussion of the annual risk assessment and annual work planning process. There is a logical linkage here: Department-level monitoring identifies potential problem areas. This information should be gathered and included in your annual risk assessment. Depending on the level of risk, the issue is placed on the annual work plan so that it can be addressed via a more formal audit process. That audit then leads to corrective action, process changes, education, and re-auditing, as necessary.

Do you have to personally complete all of these tasks? No, not you alone, although the more you are directly involved, the better your understanding of the organization and its various challenges. As I said in the beginning, a compliance officer is not an expert on every topic. That said, an established framework for working with the various functional areas must be in place to ensure that all risk areas are routinely monitored and audited at some routine frequency. We talk more below about what this element of a compliance program actually looks like. Suffice it to say, it's important to know you need a policy to highlight this element of the program and to reference specific areas that will be reviewed routinely.

If you need inspiration, look at the OIG guidance that most closely applies to your organization and any Special Fraud Alerts the OIG has issued relating to your line of business. Even documents that were published many years ago are still relevant.

### *Overpayments*

Overpayments are a significant risk area if not handled appropriately. Under the Affordable Care Act, a failure to return identified overpayments to government programs within sixty days of identification can constitute a False Claims Act violation. One question that comes up relates to overpayments by private payers, such as Blue Cross/Blue Shield. Some organizations basically don't worry about refunding such overpayments unless the patient or payer requests a refund. I do not recommend this approach.

The whole issue of overpayments calls to my mind one of those lessons from kindergarten: Don't keep what doesn't belong to you. I find it hard to defend the practice of holding onto money that should not have been paid to your organization, for whatever reason. It's also called stealing, but be careful about stating that quite so bluntly!

Your policy statement here is quite simple:

> It is the policy of Company X to refund any overpayments to government healthcare programs within sixty days of identification and to refund any overpayments by private payers in accordance with the payer's requirements.

One wrinkle here bears mentioning. Credit balances, which occur under a variety of circumstances, have specific quarterly reporting and refunding requirements. So, whereas identified overpayments must be refunded within sixty days of identification, credit balances can go up to ninety days. The courts have not definitively settled this discrepancy, as of the date of this writing; but I can tell you the ways it is currently being handled (and there may be other approaches that I'm not aware of).

Some organizations screen credit balances that are due to government payers and handle them right away in order to meet the sixty-day requirement. Other organizations handle credit balances in accordance with the regulations pertaining to credit balances and call that good. My view, when I consider the actual risk, is that an organization that is doing a good job working its credit balances is not going to be accused of retaining overpayments. If, on the other hand, the organization isn't managing credit balances properly, and government funds are sitting there not being worked, there is more likely a problem. That's my opinion; I am not a judge, obviously, so you can't rely on this as support for that practice. It's a good issue to float with legal counsel, if you're not comfortable.

My approach is to consider the actual risk and what seems to be a reasonable approach and interpretation. How to handle timely credit refunds really depends on the organization, though, because I don't believe the government is going to call credit balances a False Claims Act violation in the absence of other issues. In other words, if you're already in trouble, the government is less likely to give you a break on the issue of credit balance repayments that exceed sixty days.

Credit balance issues aside, the overpayment scenario may seem straightforward. Operationally, however, it gets complicated. You need to identify all the avenues through which the organization can learn of and manage overpayments. It is not only a question of who collects the mail from government payers. It is also a question of who in the organization can identify overpayments. In a small organization, whose responsibility this is may be very simple to ascertain: It's the billing manager or the compliance officer, for instance. In a large health system or hospital, however, it becomes more complex. Think about who conducts reviews, audits, quality control, and other activities that examine documentation, coding, billing, claims, and other payments and receipts.

Internal Audit does reviews. Quality and Risk Management people are in a position to know about issues that can result in overpayments. Compliance, of course, should be getting notice of any activities that are problematic, or potentially problematic, if the various functions are well educated about reporting expectations. A call can come in from the hotline, too. A pattern of denials or a series of record requests from a payer can indicate a problem. These are just a few examples; potential problems can make themselves known in multiple ways.

One question that naturally arises relates to our duty to investigate a "potential" overpayment. The

Affordable Care Act and its subsequent regulations do not actually say how long it should take an organization to confirm a potential overpayment; it only states that overpayments must be repaid within sixty days of identification. After some very conservative court rulings related to when the clock starts ticking, the CMS Final Rule clarified that identification occurs when the provider "has, or should have, through the exercise of reasonable diligence, determined that the person has received an overpayment and quantified the amount of the overpayment."

The "reasonable diligence" requirement means that organizations are expected to have proactive processes in place to identify overpayments, and certainly to research suspected overpayments. This is one more argument for having a robust compliance program, in case you still need to convince skeptical leaders.

Another related process to keep in mind is prevention. Overpayments can largely be avoided through a variety of proactive process improvement efforts, from vigorous front-end registration procedures that capture the correct payer information, to strong monitoring that surfaces issues before they become overpayments. Here, discuss the options with your Compliance Committee so you can identify methods for reviewing processes before problems develop.

Last, in the event your organization ends up with credit balances or overpayments for which a refund is not possible (for instance, it is money owed to a patient who cannot be located), the organization doesn't get to "keep" that money. State laws, commonly known as "escheat" laws, advise organizations on how to manage those funds. Not everyone is aware of these requirements, but the penalties can be serious if they are not followed.

### *Communication and Hotline Policy*

Communication is an expected element of a compliance program. A communication policy addresses the ability of employees to report concerns. It includes a statement delineating the organization's expectations about employees reporting identified concerns and emphasizing that retaliation is never permitted related to reporting and cooperating in investigations. The policy statement should also list the options available to employees in the organization. Those options typically include reporting to, in this order:

1. The employee's supervisor or leadership
2. Human Resources
3. The compliance officer
4. The organization's hotline

The policy may state that the organization has an open-door policy, as well. If the hotline allows for anonymous reports, you should include that language, with the caveat that the organization will protect anonymity to the extent possible. You can't guarantee anonymity because your investigation, or legal issues related to the complaint, could make it impossible to keep the complainant's identity anonymous.

In the section on procedures, be sure to include basic guidance regarding the hotline. For instance, if the hotline is managed by a third-party vendor, you should explain that. In addition, people are often worried about who is involved in reviewing their complaint, so it's a good idea to explain the process at a high level.

Hotline reports, in summary fashion, are often included in the compliance officer's reports to the board, so you may want to reference this fact, as well, in the policy. It is always useful for employees to understand what is reported to the board, and it reinforces the importance of the hotline's function.

For a large organization, you can develop a separate procedure manual that guides the individuals who may be involved in investigations. I provide more details about those processes in the section on implementing communication and the hotline element.

### *Education and Training Policy*

In the compliance program, you need a policy on compliance education and training. This is a basic policy that at a minimum states that the organization provides compliance and privacy education at new employee orientation and annually thereafter. Compliance and privacy education is mandatory, and participation is a condition of employment.

Also state that role-based training is required for some individuals based on their roles in the organization. Some obvious examples include coding and billing.

Last, education needs to be tracked and monitored. Regardless of how you roll it out, the content and attendance must be documented, so state this requirement in the policy.

You don't have to state the medium through which you will provide compliance and privacy education (in person, online, etc.), unless you know what you will be doing ahead of time. The format of the education sessions depends on the size of the organization and the budget. Different formats have different advantages, which we discuss later.

### *Internal Investigations and Corrective Actions Policy and Procedure*

A policy and procedure is expected for internal investigations and corrective actions. This policy can save a compliance officer a lot of grief in the long run. The policy statement should include language such as follows:

> It is the policy of Company X to promptly and objectively investigate any alleged

> violation of laws, regulations, or Company X policies. In the event violations are confirmed, it is the policy of Company X to develop a comprehensive corrective action plan to remedy any identified issues, including the prompt repayment of any overpayments.

Note that the policy statement itself may be generic, but it does capture the essence of what is needed.

The procedures in this document are valuable. Although approval of an investigation policy doesn't typically cause much controversy, this policy can become essential when you actually must conduct an investigation. This is decidedly true in larger organizations, where you may not know everyone well. If you have to investigate a concern in a department where the manager or the director doesn't know you, it is more likely this leader will demand to see your process. This person will want to know why you are investigating, who raised a concern, and how much you are going to disrupt their operations. Depending on the culture and size of the organization, as well as that person's opinion of Compliance, your ability to conduct the investigation can go smoothly or not, so you want a solid procedure in place.

For this document, having input from Legal and certain operational stakeholders is useful so that you don't create more problems than you are trying to resolve. A key aspect not to forget is notification. Who you need to notify, and how, in advance of an investigation is fundamental to this process. If the people who believe they need to know are not informed in advance … let's just say, it's not pretty. This lack of notification can erode their trust in you.

# TRAINING AND EDUCATION

Training and education are critical components of a compliance program for many reasons. Not only does the government expect to see a training and education program implemented, but also this element serves to protect the organization when something does go wrong. With a good compliance education and awareness program in place, with training well documented, in all likelihood any incidents will arise from either a rogue employee or a mistake of some sort. This is a far better outcome than a finding that the organization failed to train its people on appropriate practices. If a compliance incident or breach were to occur, the organization would face a situation in which it is perceived as a "bad actor"; or, at the least, a not-very-good corporate citizen, which is a far more damning verdict than being perceived as an organization that experienced an incident despite all preventive measures.

When you think about it, this is a key area where the U.S. Sentencing Guidelines are quite logically tied to a compliance program. If preventive steps were not taken and, in fact, criminal conduct occurred, you can see the linkage between conduct and sentencing. Nobody wants the organization to get into trouble, but in reality that sometimes happens, even in well-run institutions. The very best outcome in such a case is to be able to show that proper steps were made to reasonably prevent violations of laws and regulations.

Although you may have a beautiful Code of Conduct and a lovely policy manual, if people are not trained effectively, or if that training has not been documented, all the policies in the world won't help you. They might actually make the situation worse, because the presence of policies indicates that you knew what should have been done, but then failed to do it. Ignorance is no excuse; providing evidence that you knew better is not helpful, either.

So, what is the best way to roll out a compliance and privacy training program? First, let's take a quick step back to discuss the situation in which you are implementing a brand-new program, either in an organization that has never had one or in a new organization. I want to start here because this is where the foundation must be laid. When you start a new program, you don't just implement new employee education and annual education right off (you might jump to this step if you are updating an existing program). In a new program, the first part of compliance education is creating understanding of the program itself.

This begins, naturally, with the board. Educating the board is important, because the board ultimately leads the organization and must be engaged and understand what the compliance program is, why it exists, and what activities it will undertake. As you implement various pieces of the program, you will find yourself explaining that the compliance program is approved by the board and answers to the board. This eliminates some of the arguments you may have with management, but you do need to engage the board before you can make that claim.

Boards also have varying levels of experience with compliance programs. I have encountered board members who had no idea what a compliance program should do, and I have met others who relished getting into lengthy and detailed discussions of various fraud and abuse statutes. So, keep in mind that board members are people, too, with varying backgrounds, and you need them to understand and to be on your side.

With that in mind, your first foray into the boardroom as a compliance officer should be to introduce members of the board to the basics of a compliance program, including its function, necessity, and some high-level points of your plan to get the program started. Keep in mind that some of those initial activities will require board approval, so it's a good idea to give them advance warning. For example, you will start with a Code of Conduct if one isn't already in place. Or you may start with an assessment of the existing program or how the organization currently handles compliance matters; you will be expected to return to the board with results and recommendations. The CEO will give you direction and insight, so these are just some ideas.

The OIG has issued guidance regarding the role of the board and board education. It is an excellent idea to review these documents in advance of any board meetings.

The other part of a general compliance awareness campaign includes employees and other agents of the organization. The CEO or other leadership can help you identify who to work with, but a good idea is to craft a message from your CEO introducing the compliance officer and generally stating support for the compliance program. The medium of this communication depends on your organization: It may be included in a newsletter, on the intranet site, or by some other mechanism. Don't wait for your executive to take the lead on this, because he or she may not think of it. Your job is top of mind to you, but not necessarily to others, so don't take it personally; but also don't be afraid to speak up and ask how best to introduce yourself and the program to the organization. It's important to start out on the right foot.

Another effective way to become part of the organization—which is really what you are working on here—is to find out which leadership or executive teams you should be introduced to and then make the acquaintance. Again, depending on the organization, an executive team, a Medical Executive Committee, or a less formal group might be prominent stakeholders. You may find other leadership teams important to infiltrate, such as Human Resources and Revenue Cycle. In a small organization, this may not apply because the same people cover all the functions. The point is to get yourself inserted into the influential groups so that you can inform them of your activities and how each function may be involved or affected. This is also a good chance to learn about their perspectives, so you can start identifying allies and those who will require extra effort to engage.

Don't shortchange the significance of this initial process of getting in front of your stakeholders. It benefits you in the long run in a variety of ways. One strategy I can't recommend too strongly is to spend more time listening than talking. Give people the basic information about the compliance program, and then ask them for their input—the biggest benefit here. Depending on the group, ask about compliance activities that intersect with their functions. For instance, with Human Resources, let them know you will be implementing a hotline. Ask them how complaints have been managed in the past and their thoughts on the best way to work together in this area. You can ask a Medical Executive Committee what would work best, in terms of media and timing, to provide the medical staff with compliance education.

The concept here is to listen to what people say and how they say it. This is a golden opportunity to assess how you can work with specific groups, how supportive they will be, and what their needs, strengths, and weaknesses may be. You cannot, however, allow these groups to tell you how to do your job—there will be times when they push back against your recommendations—but the fact that you ask them questions and listen for responses goes a long way toward showing that you want to work collaboratively, not force your program down their throats. Demonstrate that you want to be a resource for them and that your goal is to support what they do, not dictate how they do it. You are there to help them make sure they are carrying out their functions in a way that keeps them out of trouble.

You may be getting the sense that I focus a lot on relationship building as part of compliance education, and you're right. In organizations where the compliance officer fails to integrate into the institution and to build the right culture, compliance education becomes merely a "check the box" activity that doesn't do much to support actual compliance. In organizations where, on the other hand, the compliance officer engages leaders, the message to employees is that compliance is important, and it is who they are as a company. Employees pick up on this, and their level of engagement will reflect that of their leaders.

So, once you have done all of the preliminary meets and greets, it's time to build your actual compliance and privacy program. You know that you need to include a new employee orientation; if you are a new employee yourself, you have hopefully just been through that process. Most of the organizations I have worked with have in-person orientation of some type, usually coordinated by Human Resources, and various functional areas provide their own training. Areas often represented include employee health, information security, compliance and privacy, any function that must orient employees to the way the organization is run, the rules and expectations, and the key policies that affect their work. Specific types of employees, such as medical and nursing staff, undergo additional training or orientation. In a small practice, of course, you will just get shown to your desk in all likelihood!

Your first stop, then, is with the Human Resource person who manages new employee orientation. Find out how often orientation is done and how long a spot you can have on the schedule. You need at least a half hour, and more time is better but may not be easy to obtain, depending on the calendar. The HR person will probably want you to prepare a presentation that can be cued up and ready to go when you speak. *Practice tip: Verify your presentation is integrated into the program at least the day before the training.* In one instance, I expected my presentation to be loaded and ready; but the person coordinating training somehow skipped it, and I ended up talking through the presentation from my printed slides. It was okay, but not optimal. Lesson learned: Don't make any assumptions about this.

A different set of circumstances that deserves to be acknowledged, since I have referenced many large organization issues, is the challenges of implementing compliance programs in very small offices or practices. If you are designated as a compliance officer in that situation, you are most likely also the office manager, Human Resources department, and perhaps cover several other areas, too. When you have multiple roles and work in a close environment, it is difficult to keep your colleagues mindful of the multiple hats you wear. In small offices, people are more familiar and more casual. Doing your compliance job is certainly easier to the extent you aren't managing a massive project across multiple locations and departments, but you must realize that the same requirements apply. You still need to make sure everyone is educated about compliance and privacy and that you keep a record of it.

### *New Employee Orientation*

Once your organization understands what a compliance program is, it's time to start rolling out the actual program. Realistically, in organizations big enough to have ongoing hiring, you want to start new employee orientation as soon as you can. You can design this session as soon as you have a Code of Conduct, because that document sets out the organizational standards. You don't need every policy written and approved in order to properly orient new employees to compliance and privacy. I will add, however, that if you see a challenge in getting the Code completed timely, go forward with your content and update later with Code references. New employees have to get orientation.

Your orientation program will typically be about a half hour long; if you can get more time, you are fortunate. As you design the presentation, keep two things in mind: First, new employees are bombarded with session after session of orientation, which often becomes tedious and tiring for them. Second, given the first point, you want to divulge only the most important points that all employees should know. Your goal in orientation is not to make new hires into compliance experts; rather, provide them with key points they need to be aware of. If you can keep your presentation from being boring, given your audience's orientation overload, there is a better chance they will remember who you are and a few points you mention.

First, include a brief introduction to compliance programs in general and yours in particular. I don't recommend droning on too long about the seven elements and the OIG, although it doesn't hurt to at least let them know why we have compliance programs. The most important information is what you want them to do, not do, and be aware of.

Once you set the stage, introduce them to the organization's Code of Conduct. You can actually tie most of the presentation to this document. Usually, orientation packets include a copy of the Code (discuss this with Human Resources in advance to ensure that the Code is included), so you can even have them follow along in the Code document while you talk, if you want. The Code really includes most of the key points you need to cover for compliance: overall expectations of integrity, non-retaliation, fraud and abuse, conflicts of interest, excluded providers, accurate documentation, coding and billing, and privacy. If the Code is in development, it's fine to say that, but include the key topics and talking points that you know will apply. New employees also need to know that there is a hotline or a mechanism that enables them to voice concerns and how to use it. Those are the key pieces to include.

You can make your presentation interesting by incorporating a couple of stopping points and quizzing the group: Ask them to give an example of something easy, like a privacy violation or fraud and abuse. I like to do this because I know they are probably bored at this point (unless you get a morning time slot, which I recommend. Scheduling your bit right before lunch is inopportune because, if things run late, you are between them and a break. If you are right after lunch, they may come straggling back, texting, sleepy, etc.), and posing a question can invigorate their minds. A good way to start the orientation is by letting them know you will be quizzing them, so they should try to stay awake. A comment like that, I believe, lets them know they must pay some degree of attention and that you know they are fried from sitting there all day. It also usually gets a laugh or two, which is always good for a compliance officer!

The more you can talk through the presentation and give relevant examples, the better they will remember the salient points. People remember stories more than lists and policies. Give true-to-life examples of what you are talking about, for each issue, and your presentation will be more effective and less boring for attendees. Compliance doesn't have to be dry and dull—some parts are highly dramatic!—so set that tone from the beginning and you are starting them off on the right foot.

A main objective of orientation, besides giving them general knowledge and introducing yourself, is making sure they know where to go for answers. You can even make this one of your audience-involvement questions: If you have a question about a compliance issue, where do you get the answer? (a) Intranet site, (b) Compliance officer, (c) Code of Conduct, or (d) All of the above. Not too difficult, right? But it does reinforce the point. We don't need people to know all the answers; we need them to have an idea of when to ask a question, and where to go for the answer.

If your session is right before a break, it's a good idea to hang around afterward; often people have questions they want to ask, but not in a group setting. If they ask about a policy you haven't worked through yet, it's fine to tell them that you are still building the new program and haven't approached that subject yet. Just be sure to make a note of topics you are asked about, because they might be worth considering while you are policy writing. New employees bring their own experiences to the company, and sometimes they are good resources for ideas and different perspectives.

### *Annual Education*

Another part of a compliance and privacy education program is annual education. The size of the organization and the resources available to Compliance dictate how you will conduct yearly employee education.

In a very small practice, you can do education in a team meeting. In-person education has the advantage of being inexpensive and allows for dialogue. The downside is that you need to make sure everyone participates, so depending on the size of the workforce, that may be a challenge. Expect that you will need to supply some makeup opportunity. For in-person education, keep a sign-in sheet and retain it along with a copy of the presentation. This provides evidence of training.

An option commonly used for annual education is online education. How this is done varies widely: You can sign up with a vendor that provides compliance and privacy education, you can do it yourself, or you can employ some combination of the two, such as hiring a vendor to host the platform where you can add content. I prefer the latter option, because I think it's important to include your organization's specific information, especially material on the hotline number, the compliance officer's name and contact information, and the Code of Conduct. Having some prepackaged modules can be helpful, though, especially for topics such as privacy and security, where the rules are set and there isn't much need for creativity or customization (except when it comes to your organization's specific practices and the state laws).

One benefit of online education is that it's trackable, and it's easy to get reports on who has completed the training. Depending on the system, you can even send reminders to those who have yet to complete the education. Chasing people with reminders can become cumbersome, especially in a large organization, so this benefit is not to be taken lightly. It's effective when the system escalates reminders, sending them to the individual's boss after so many attempts—it saves you a lot of legwork and prevents you having to threaten people. Annual education is a condition of employment; noncompliance is reported to leadership and to the Compliance Committee. Employees need to understand this from the get-go, so there are no surprises.

You do need to be mindful of other "mandatories." Different types of employees have various other mandatory education they are required to complete each year, and usually it's all due at the end of the year. Pulling people off the floor to do hours of education can aggravate management. Also, some people don't have access to computers so they must use a shared workstation or do the training on their own time, which raises another set of issues. From a logistics perspective, you can see why heaps of annual education can become a sore point.

When you set up your schedule, consider the following ways you can make this requirement more palatable for management: You can coordinate your mandatories with other organization-wide mandatory education so it's done in one shot. Or you can find out what time frame is most acceptable and create an alternate schedule around that. There is no reason you can't require your mandatories to be due by the end of June instead of December. You will score points early on if you discuss this with managers and your

Compliance Committee to demonstrate that you respect their scheduling issues and are asking for input. This is another way to seek collaboration instead of cramming it down their throats.

With respect to timing, not everyone will complete the education by the deadline. With that in mind, roll it out well in advance of the due date and expect that you will be chasing certain individuals for a month or two (maybe more) afterward.

In terms of content, be sure to include the basics every time. Refresh employees on the Code of Conduct, the hotline, fraud and abuse, and the other core policies. Privacy, as well, requires some in-depth coverage, because this is a big risk area and potentially affects everyone.

The challenge with annual education is keeping it fresh. A best practice is to update it every year. You may not change much content, but include regulatory updates, issues that have come up in the organization, hotline trends, or other happenings to keep the training timely and relevant. Annual training is one of those "check the box" activities, but that doesn't mean it has to be painful for employees. Education modules that include some form of quiz or test is optimal, and again, it should be updated every year. You might be surprised to learn that employees do remember the content and quizzes, and will note if it never changes.

### *Role-Based Education*

Role-based education is not necessary for everyone, but it is important for individuals who work in high-risk areas where mistakes are costly.

An obvious example is coding and billing. Be completely sure that coders and billers are well trained not only on the general standards for doing their work, but also on the organization's related policies and procedures, such as fraud and abuse prevention and other compliance topics. The good news is that employees with certifications, like certified coders, must participate in ongoing education to maintain their credentials. This is true for most licensed or credentialed staff, which makes your job easier to some extent.

People who handle patient medical and financial records also need role-based training. The Health Insurance Portability and Accountability Act (HIPAA) specifically calls out the expectation about role-based training, which means you need to think about which employees occupy positions that should receive additional training. People who handle release of information (ROI) are an important example. They need to understand critical issues like who they can release records to, what documentation is required, which verification procedures are in place, and how to manage patient requests.

If you're building a new program in a large organization, talk to people to get a sense of where the organization might have points of vulnerability. For instance, a large hospital might maintain records in more than one place. Does the clinic use a different records system from the emergency department? It's smart to identify as many of these issues as you can on the front end as you are designing the education program and choosing the audiences. What about joint ventures? Do you have any responsibilities there? Make sure you have a handle on this, if you are in a large organization.

Role-based training can be managed through online modules or in department meetings. Consider attending department meetings in these high-risk areas for this purpose, and because people in these functions will have questions for you when you show up that might not otherwise come to your attention. A lot of people won't come looking for you or send an email about issues they think probably aren't a "big deal," but they will ask if you show up. This is an ongoing informal part of compliance education that should be baked in to your routine job. Making sure people know you and routinely see you around greatly improves the chances that you hear about little things before they become big things.

People who are involved in managing contracts are good candidates for role-based training, too. With all the risks associated with financial arrangements, it is crucial that those who manage contracts, as well as the individuals involved in the actual contracting, have a true understanding of the various risks. No need for them to become Stark and Anti-Kickback experts, but they must generally understand how those issues can arise and when to seek Legal or Compliance advice. Part of their education reinforces the importance of effectively managing contracts. Compliance risks bubble to the surface when contracts are not appropriately reviewed or renewed, so a tracking system must be in place, as well as a process for keeping documents compliant.

### *Physicians*

Physicians and other providers who document in patient medical records must be trained on documentation standards. This includes residents at teaching facilities. Accurate documentation is critical for both compliance and revenue reasons, as well as for the obvious patient care concern.

Although not every physician who comes into the organization will have challenges with documentation, a best practice—one that pays for itself in the long run—is to review each provider's documentation when they are hired. If you can set up a process that includes a review of their charting and then provides education on their weak areas, it will benefit the organization tremendously. This process can be baked in to the organization and can be presented as a freebie.

You need physicians to buy in to the idea that good documentation is critical and that they are getting free assistance in this area.

Try to cultivate a physician champion or encourage the Medical Staff office to be a cheerleader for you and the value you can provide, so that the program is all the much easier to implement. Physicians are typically competitive and want to be at the top of their game, which can work to your advantage if you sell it right. If you can't get with new physicians during their initial ninety days, at least make sure they get on the list for a routine documentation audit during their first year. Don't wait too long, however, because a physician with a real documentation problem can cause a repayment problem or other compliance issues. Better to find an issue sooner and nip it in the bud.

If you are in a large organization, it is important to make the Medical Staff office your first stop in planning physician compliance activities. Make sure you have a solid understanding of employed physicians, contracted, and credentialed only. This will largely determine not only what forums you can tap into, but also how much leverage you have. In terms of education, I have heard some compliance officers were able to get continuing medical education (CME) credits for their compliance training. Ask about this possibility when you meet with the Medical Staff leader to discuss the compliance program activities for physicians.

You can learn from them how to do that, which does provide valuable motivation for physicians. Free food is an additional strategy that works with the doctors and clinical staff (not to mention residents, they are always looking for a meal!).

One last strategy to consider, no matter how large your organization: Try to locate a physician "champion" for compliance. Having one of their own support your efforts definitely gives you an advantage. Ask Medical Staff about this, as well. The beauty of having a physician champion is that you will find them siding with you when one of the clinicians becomes argumentative or challenges you (yes, it will probably happen). It's especially valuable if your champion is in an influential role, such as the chair of the Medical Executive Committee or is generally well-respected. Unless you are a physician yourself, you will never have that extra level of credibility on your own. That doesn't mean you can't be successful without a physician sidekick, but it's a huge benefit, if you can pull it off.

# AUDITING AND MONITORING

Auditing and monitoring are critical components of effective compliance programs. The first point is to understand the difference between the two; these are not interchangeable terms.

Auditing is usually conducted by someone outside of the functional area, perhaps even outside of the company, such as a consultant or accounting firm. Most organizations have an accounting firm conduct annual audits. Audits are typically reported to the board or perhaps to an executive team, depending on the type of audit. Audits can be conducted as routine business, like the annual audit performed by an accounting firm, or they can be conducted based on specific issues.

Monitoring, on the other hand, is ongoing review typically performed by the process owner or on behalf of an individual in the business unit. For example, a billing manager might routinely pull a selection of bills that are ready to be released and verify that they are correct. The key points to understand about monitoring is that it is ongoing, less formal, and typically doesn't result in any detailed reporting, although the process should be documented.

Both auditing and monitoring serve purposes that are important to the compliance program. Keep in mind that it is not necessarily your job to actually *do* either of these activities, but you must occupy a central role in the auditing process and be in the loop on the monitoring process.

Monitoring is an activity that most departments are probably already doing in some form or fashion, even if you are not aware of it. As you get settled into your role, explore this area with the various department heads you meet with. Think about each area in advance of that conversation to identify areas that you think should be part of an ongoing monitoring process. For instance, before you meet with Human Resources, think about which processes it should be monitoring. Many laws and regulations affect the department, but some are more relevant from a compliance perspective than others. A key issue to discuss is how HR verifies that no excluded individuals are hired. How does the department document that? Many companies, particularly larger ones, outsource this function along with background checks. If that is the case, what documentation does the vendor provide as a paper trail?

Temporary and per diem employees present a variety of potential challenges to an organization. As the compliance officer, you need to get a handle on how these employees are hired, screened, and trained before they join the organization. It may seem like a relatively easy task—just check the contract with the organization, right? You also must ensure that these types of employees are provided training in compliance and privacy. The organization must also do excluded provider screening and background checks.

You may find that temporary and per diem employees are not brought in through Human Resources, and, in fact, Human Resources has no idea who they are. Some departments might hire temporary employees as a routine matter of course. Consider Nursing, for example. Nursing departments frequently manage their own staffing levels and have agencies they use. Are contracts in place that cover the compliance issues necessary to protect the organization? And, if so, does anyone check (monitor) to verify that employees adhere to the terms of their agreement?

Monitoring becomes much more challenging when you start considering scenarios such as this. First, who are all the people coming into the organization? And, second, who is minding the store with respect to their compliance with the various agreements? Is anyone even reviewing the agreements with an eye toward compliance? This is a significant area for monitoring; and in a large organization, the more you start exploring it, the more different permutations you will uncover.

I must mention another related scenario while we're on the topic of monitoring employees who aren't "regular" employees. The organization may have outsourced entire functions, such as coding, billing, or other clinical units. It might have, for instance, contracted with a practice group to staff the emergency department. Those contracts are generally tracked more closely because they exist at the corporate level and are not entered into by a department head.

Even so, if the compliance officer was not involved in the contracting process, the agreement may contain issues that you should know about, like the ones previously mentioned. Even contracts that cover background screening, training and education, licensure, and so forth must be subjected to some level of verification or monitoring of these risk areas. What happens if the outside organization brings in a new employee? Does your organization know about the hire? Do new employees receive training? Explore these areas, and chances are good that you will find such compliance issues are not consistently addressed across your organization, because different services are handled differently. Physician groups are not handled in the same way as the health information management function, for instance. You will work with different stakeholders to uncover these issues.

It's good to be aware of the range of issues that the organization faces in terms of auditing and monitoring. For example, if you are at a teaching facility, how are residents and students background-checked? What about volunteers? If you are at a small organization, you can read this and be grateful this level of complication doesn't apply to you. But chances are good that someday you will end up at a larger place, so know the risk areas that need to be monitored across the range of organization types. Students can be challenging cats to herd, because if you are in a large organization, you may find that there are many different areas with students, and they may have their own staff member who coordinates onboarding those students. The rehabilitation group might have one process, but nursing has a different one, for instance. What is provided by the school, according to the contract? Some may be very rigorous with respect to screening and training, etc., whereas others may have bare minimum agreements. What happens if you identify issues with the student's performance, from a compliance perspective? The agreements should address that issue, which will come up if you identify issues during auditing or monitoring.

Next, let's consider how the coding and billing functions should be monitored. In a small organization, a conversation with one person can uncover how coders and billers are trained, whether they are certified, and how their work is monitored to ensure accuracy. In large hospitals or health systems, you must consider the different types of coders: inpatient, outpatient, and coders for different specialty areas. For areas with outsourced functions, like the emergency department, how do they manage coding and billing? Where are medical records maintained? Does one EMR span the organization, or do different departments use different systems and processes, or a hybrid model? As you dig into the questions around routine monitoring, you will likely discover more than one answer if you are in a large organization. My purpose here is to help you think about these issues so that you aren't caught unawares. Even a small organization can have different arrangements that you will uncover, so it's important to assume nothing. It's easy to overlook some discrete aspect of your business unless you conduct your own due diligence to ascertain who is doing what, who is responsible ultimately, and what protections exist in the contracts.

As I said earlier, the thing about monitoring is that you should be in the loop. Though the various departments obviously do not report to you, they should provide you with information on their monitoring activities, issues they identify, and steps they take to address them. You can and should be involved in the corrective actions if they are compliance issues.

This highlights the benefits of having a compliance liaison in different departments. These individuals help coordinate monitoring and compliance activities and make sure you are informed without creating significant extra work for you. Here's the important point about monitoring: Monitoring systems are probably already in place in the various organizational areas; you just want to be informed and engaged if a problem arises. If monitoring is not already occurring, particularly in high-risk areas, then thank goodness a compliance officer is now available, because someone needs to make sure the process gets started.

Coding and billing are only as good as the documentation they are based on. A coder can only code to what is documented, so there are two issues here. First, whether the coder is accurately coding based on the documentation should be reviewed. Second, an ongoing review process should ensure that the documentation is capturing everything that it should. One way a compliance officer can bring revenue to the table is by identifying documentation shortcomings that result in lost money. Especially now, with ICD-10, when so much more detail is necessary in order to bill for the full amount for the services performed.

As I mentioned earlier, physician documentation should be subject to ongoing monitoring. Although it can be resource-intensive to adequately monitor documentation, this one area directly correlates to revenues and compliance. For this reason, you may have no problem acquiring resources for this function as opposed to other areas of compliance. You can explain that better documentation not only means the organization can bill for more, but also it reduces the likelihood that overpayments will occur. Nobody likes overpayments, and now there is a strict requirement that they be paid back quickly.

Monitoring should occur for all areas with potential compliance issues, but the ones I mention here are most likely to create problems if left unattended. With that in mind, the last area I want to discuss relates to financial arrangements. The big-dollar compliance settlements and fines often relate to a violation of Stark or the Anti-Kickback statute. These situations can come up in a variety of ways. One of the most common is with medical director agreements in which the pay rate is higher than fair market value or the actual services provided appear unnecessary or perhaps are not documented. The government takes the perspective that the organization is paying the physician for referrals, which is illegal. A variation on this theme is when a hospital or health system rents space to a physician, but either rents it for a dollar amount less than fair market value, or just doesn't collect the rent. Providing free services or equipment to physicians is also unacceptable as a possible strategy for paying for referrals.

So, how do you get your arms around this? The best place to start is with the Finance department. In large organizations, you might want to engage Internal Audit to put this on the audit plan. You need to tie the payments to physicians or physician practices back to a contract. This sounds easier to do than it is, especially if it's never been done at your organization. Every payment made to physicians should be under the terms of a contract; there is no *de minimis* standard when it comes to Stark or the Anti-Kickback statute.

The recent Medicare Physician Fee Schedule for 2016 eased up some on the requirements, stating that the agreement doesn't necessarily have to be all in one document and that there can be "contemporaneous" documentation, with signatures, showing the intent of the parties. This actually makes the audit process more challenging, because when you can't locate a contract, you have to hunt for adequate documentation to piece together the relationship. It's also not clear yet how the government will actually manage this change in audits, so I do not advocate for anything less than a contract.

In your organization, you may find that small payments for such items as continuing medical education (CME) have been made with no contract. You may find expired contracts. Or you might not find an agreement, period. Even in small organizations and those that already have a solid contract management process in place, you may still find payment aberrations, but they will be far fewer. If you suspect that you may discover a lot of problems, I recommend letting your in-house attorney know in advance of the review, just so counsel can be involved and provide any necessary guidance. They may want to put the review under attorney-client privilege. Financial arrangements are such a high-risk area, you can end up with Stark violations even if the organization had no intent to enter into an inappropriate relationship. It's best to be supremely careful around this issue.

A resource that can alert you to potential problems is the Open Payments database. As mentioned earlier, the Physician Payment Sunshine Act requires all device and pharmaceutical companies to disclose gifts and payments made to physicians and teaching hospitals. Data relating to those payments is publicly available. Physicians and teaching hospitals do have the opportunity to register and review the information that will be posted online on the CMS Open Payments database. You can use this tool to see whether any physicians are on the receiving end of payments from drug or device companies. If so, there should be a conflict of interest disclosure that shows the payment, if the form includes the appropriate questions to capture that information.

You definitely want to know whether you have physicians who are heavily paid by these industries and what they are being paid for. Plenty of legitimate activities, such as research, can show up in the database, but there is also the chance that certain payments that have not been disclosed internally are problematic.

Monitoring this database is obviously another potentially resource-intensive activity, depending on the size of your organization, and I don't know that many organizations have dedicated resources to this activity yet. At a minimum, familiarize yourself with this website and learn how to use it so that you can check it quickly if a question comes up or you think there may be a problem.

# CORRECTIVE ACTIONS

Once you have policies and procedures in place and you have educated people, there is an expectation that things are being done correctly. We all know, however, that people are imperfect, and lapses and mistakes will happen. Hopefully, no problems that you identify were deliberate; but when you find out about one, the next step is to fix it, and your plan to fix it needs to be documented.

In government audits for any types of compliance violations, the best thing you can do is show a corrective action plan. You may have to self-report a problem, or the government may notify you if it identifies the issue; but in either case you want to be able to demonstrate what you are doing about it. This establishes that you are committed to doing right by correcting identified violations.

When you first become aware of a potential problem, investigate the situation to determine the scope of the concern. What was the cause? How long has it been going on? Who was involved in it? Was anyone aware of the problem, and if so, why didn't anyone report or correct it sooner? It's crucial to be able to show that you did a deep dive into an identified concern to truly understand the full nature of what went wrong and why. You can't implement a corrective action plan until you have taken this important step. And don't let the operational owner put you off with a pat answer or assurance; you need to be comfortable that you have thoroughly chased down the issue yourself.

Once you have a solid understanding of the details, you need to figure out the various steps to correct it. These activities may include creating a new policy or revising the current policy or procedure; training and education; Human Resources discipline for the responsible employee or employees; and system changes. If the issue came to you internally, you need to determine whether it requires reporting and to whom (talk to legal counsel if it looks like that may be the case).

And, last but not least, make sure you quickly identify any overpayments to government payers. As discussed earlier, all overpayments need to be repaid appropriately, and government payers have a strict time frame in which to do so. Be sure to create a written corrective action plan so that you can produce it if necessary. Assign each task an owner and document the time frame of its completion. Monitor completion of the various steps.

Be very sure that you understand the complete scope of the problem. Say, for instance, an issue is brought to your attention through the hotline. You may find that throughout the system, modifiers are automatically being attached to certain codes, creating a higher level of reimbursement. The reporting individual wants to remain anonymous because they have tried to raise this issue to their manager and have been treated badly ever since.

The first thing you do, of course, is put together a plan to investigate the issue. You know the facts, which department is impacted, and which codes are affected; so you must discover how long it's been going on, who knew about it (somebody did, it was reported!), which payers were involved, and how much money is actually at issue.

Lay out your plan and go to the department head to get more information. The first question they will ask you is who reported the issue. Then this manager quite likely will start guessing and tell you who it probably was and how that person has been causing trouble and that the issue has been taken care of. Perhaps this department head won't react this way; maybe he or she will be cooperative, but go along with me here for a minute.

You point out to the manager that it's not relevant how you heard of the issue and that you need to collect these various pieces of information. You take the opportunity to remind the department head about non-retaliation and the sixty days requirement for overpayments and that this problem needs to be resolved in a timely manner. You get the information, sooner or later, and set about fixing the issue and identifying overpayments. Perhaps you also think that education is warranted because this issue should never have gone on for so long (if that's the case).

The overpayments are managed and the erroneous modifier is remedied. Problem solved. So, you're done, right?

No, not so fast. You still have an employee who has basically been punished for raising the issue, or at least he or she believes so. If the employee never actually comes forward during your review (which can happen), then you need to think about another issue to be corrected: retaliation.

This is a difficult situation because, with the anonymity, you can't know for certain that retaliation has actually occurred. But you do know, on the basis of how the manager responded to your initial inquiry, that the manager *might* have acted inappropriately. And you heard other comments during your review that make you suspicious that the department head may have retaliated against someone. There is not enough evidence with which to discipline the manager, but the issue also can't be ignored. So, how do you handle it?

You have a few options here, depending on a variety of factors, including the individuals involved and the culture of the organization. My preference is to have a chat with Human Resources, the CEO, or both, and let them know your concerns around this issue and that you think it might be a good time for some general reeducation. If you choose to implement education, you can hold a session in a management meeting and perhaps include another common topic so that it seems routine. Make sure you document attendance. Then, if it ever comes up, you have evidence that you did what you could to reeducate.

The other, more direct approach is to talk to the manager. To do so runs the risk that the manager will assume which employee caused them grief and will somehow enact a reprisal, despite what you are saying. You really must consider the personality and behavior of the manager in question before deciding. It's fine to want to tackle these issues head-on, in theory; but if it's going to cause harm to an employee and disrupt operations, not to mention put the organization at risk, confrontation is not always the best plan (in my opinion). Think it through and maybe consult with HR; they may know the manager better than you and can suggest a way to deal fairly with the person. It's important in these situations to think about the culture of the organization, the department, and weigh the risks and benefits of your choices. It also makes a difference how much education has already been provided around retaliation. If everyone just had their annual compliance training, and non-retaliation is fully covered, then just a refresher is clearly not your best option.

In any event, you must address the retaliation concern, even if just in a management meeting, and document that you did so. Think about the employee who reported. If the manager retaliates, that employee may quit and call an attorney. You definitely don't want to have to explain later why you didn't address the retaliation issue. Plus, you don't want to contribute to a culture in which such issues are ignored and accepted. Ignoring these types of behaviors will often lead to an escalation over time, and even if you don't start out with an actual legal claim, over time the behavior will deteriorate and create a bigger risk.

The point of this example is that you must be mindful of all aspects of a complaint when you set about investigating and correcting it. You want your corrective action to get at the whole problem, not just the surface issue. Sometimes a complaint seems to be about one issue when, in fact, the person reporting has bigger concerns but wasn't sure where to start. So, listen and get as much information as you can so that you can really address the entire problem. What initially seems to be a minor blip can balloon into something much larger because the individual either doesn't understand the entire issue or is unsure or wary about saying it.

The bottom line is to document a corrective action plan that addresses all the issues raised. Add to it, if necessary, as more issues come to light during your investigation. Whereas small issues might swell into larger ones, you might also discover that a big deal is no more than a misunderstanding. The point is to thoroughly review and correct all concerns that are brought to your attention.

# COMMUNICATION

MANY BREAKDOWNS AND PROBLEMS in organizations can be traced back to a failure of communications. Compliance program challenges are no exception. When the OIG includes communications as one element of an effective compliance program, it relates in large part to the availability of reporting channels. The communication tools you need to have in place, however, are much broader than just mechanisms to submit complaints.

Let's start with reporting mechanisms. The first and most commonly implemented reporting channel is a hotline. In large organizations, management of a hotline can be outsourced, which has benefits and drawbacks. One benefit is that reporting can truly be anonymous. Call centers are trained to respond to a range of calls, and they have a consistent list of questions. Operators fill out reports based on phoned-in concerns and send them to the compliance officer (or whomever the company designates). Internal "hotlines," by comparison, might not be considered truly confidential by employees. If there are trust issues within the company, whether justified or not, you may be less likely to get calls on an internal line.

The advantage, though, to an internally managed hotline is that the person answering the calls does actually work in the company and knows the organization. So, for instance, if a caller is concerned that a specific behavior is a violation of the Code of Conduct, the compliance officer can discuss the issue directly with the caller, and perhaps put certain issues to rest right then, while educating the employee. A third-party vendor can only take the call and forward it, adding a step to the resolution process.

An advantage of outsourced hotlines is the reporting feature. Call centers usually have a tracking system that helps manage the calls and generates reports based on whatever criteria the organization wants to see. Depending on your call volume, this can be a big deal, especially if the hotline fields many calls and the board or Compliance Committee wants to see the reports routinely. In addition, most tracking tools can be used to track incidents not related to the hotline, as well; so if you outsource your hotline, you will have a reporting tool to use for all incidents. This can really streamline and automate your work.

If you work for a small practice, outsourcing a hotline might be overkill. Your challenge, then, is to create a reporting environment that employees feel comfortable using. I have witnessed, even in larger organizations, employees reluctant to be seen coming into my office. I have had to meet employees at a Starbucks or other place off-site on plenty of occasions. The key is to be available and to build trust with the employees so they feel safe coming to you.

For outsourced hotlines, you need to instruct the vendor on how to manage or triage the different types of calls. The vendor will send email alerts to the individuals responsible for specific types of issues. For example, you can have your Human Resources director receive notification of all calls pertaining to employment issues.

You are still the overall manager of the hotline process, however, and it is your responsibility to report, at a summary level, the types of calls and resolution of complaints. In addition to triaging calls by subject, you also need to set up the hotline to escalate certain types of calls. If, for instance, a caller is complaining about you, the compliance officer, your boss should be notified (and not you!). It is important to discuss escalation with the vendor to ensure that all eventualities are considered, even complaints about the CEO, CFO, general counsel, and other leadership. Typically, the board committee or board chair receives notices of those calls in order to preserve objectivity. Although the likelihood of such calls is remote, it is important that employees know that the process is in place to address any type of complaint.

A specific argument related to Human Resources issues invariably arises when it comes to the hotline. Employees frequently use compliance hotlines to report concerns about discrimination, scheduling fairness, and other HR-related problems. At some point in your compliance career, you will be confronted either by Human Resources or someone on the executive team about the appropriateness of HR calls coming to the compliance hotline. Let me share with you how I respond to those concerns.

First, the compliance hotline is a safety net for the organization. It is inappropriate to tell employees that they cannot use the hotline for raising any type of concern. You do not want to discourage employees from using an anonymous reporting option. Second, the HR-type issues will typically be triaged to Human Resources to investigate, unless the allegations are directly about that department. You, as the compliance officer, are the process owner and as such will be monitoring all complaints to make sure they are appropriately managed and reported. This is an appropriate role for the compliance officer and creates a system of checks and balances.

Some people object strongly to this structure, which is why I am warning you so you are prepared for "corporate bullies" who may try to find a way to circumvent the hotline for HR or other types of issues. Mostly, they just don't understand the full purpose of the hotline, although sometimes it is also a turf issue.

That leads me to the next facet of communication: an "open-door" policy for employees to report, and education for management and Human Resources about the handling of employees who report compliance concerns. As we have discussed with respect to retaliation, managers can easily respond badly to an employee's concerns, and the result can be disastrous for the organization.

When you create policies and communications around the issue of retaliation, it is vital that everyone understands the need to treat compliance concerns seriously and to pass them along to you, even if the employee is aggravating or incorrect. The issue is that an employee who thinks there is a compliance problem and who believes the organization doesn't care is more likely to go outside of the company to report it. This is particularly true if employees believe they are being retaliated against for raising the issue.

As I have explained to many HR and management staff, even if the employee's concern is not valid, you don't want the government to be invited to come investigate the company. There is just no way that is a good outcome, even if no problems are identified. Potential whistleblowers are often created by poor communication, retaliation (or the perception of retaliation), and inadequate resolution of reported concerns.

My view is that you can't overeducate management about these issues. No matter how much I have preached about listening to and taking seriously employees who have concerns, I still end up with employees coming to me with stories of bad behavior by management. There are multiple reasons for this, including personality conflicts, a perception by managers that employees are trying to cause trouble or undermine them, or a simple lack of management training. Managers may believe employees are being critical of them and are getting them in trouble by reporting, so they react badly. Because I have seen this, in various forms, pretty consistently over the years, I can't overstate the significance of this issue.

Another aspect of communication to keep in mind is confidentiality. Employees who report issues to you may be concerned that someone will find out about the reporting. Whether the concern is well founded or not, you need to be very sensitive to this issue. Confidentiality is tricky to maintain because, if you need to investigate an issue, others will speculate about how the concern came to your attention. They may even ask you outright. Or the manager may say something like, "It was Jane who reported this, wasn't it? She is always complaining ..." And, of course, you can't confirm or deny, but just the fact that you are investigating an issue similar to one this specific employee already raised may be revealing.

When employees comes to you with concerns over confidentiality, you need to be honest with them. Let them know that you will respect their wish for confidentiality to the extent that you can. You can't promise absolute anonymity, because if the issue is serious enough, a time may come when you have to self-report, and the information they have may be critical. In addition, if it is known that a certain person has already raised a specific concern, people will jump to the obvious conclusion about who went to the compliance officer.

At this point, as you discuss confidentiality with employees, you can remind them that retaliation will not be tolerated. Also, you need to work to establish trust with them if you don't already have a solid relationship. It is essential that you make them understand that if they experience any type of retribution or think that anything inappropriate is happening as a result of their reporting, they come to you.

In the event they do come to you with such a retaliation concern, part of earning their trust comes from how you handle the situation. Again, I would start by having a conversation with Human Resources.

Work with the department to do whatever is necessary to protect employees from retaliation and make sure management understands. Handling it this way is especially important when you are a new compliance officer, because your response will be discussed among employees, and word will get around whether they can or cannot trust you. If employees come to trust you, more may show up in your office, even if just to ask questions. If they don't trust you, the silence will be deafening.

You need to rectify retaliation concerns without making an enemy of HR or management, which can be tricky. If, however, management has truly been treating the employee badly, they need to be held accountable in no uncertain terms, and you must have a conversation with your CEO about it.

Those are the key points regarding the reporting aspect of communication. But a compliance officer has to do more than just keep an open door to effectively communicate. Employees need to be aware of reporting options and should have compliance and privacy reminders in their environment regularly. We have already talked about education, which is obviously a key piece of communication. Ongoing awareness is another aspect that is never-ending. An effective compliance program should have an awareness campaign that constantly evolves and involves fresh techniques to get employees' attention.

In an awareness campaign, a few items should always be front and center: Posters reminding employees about the hotline should be visible in all areas where employees congregate, such as break rooms. Also hang posters reminding everyone about the importance of patient privacy and information security. If you are a creative type, you can create your own, or you can buy them from various vendors.

As you know, people become accustomed to objects in their environment and at some point no longer notice them. For that reason, keep your reminders fresh and ever-changing, move them around, and update the message. You can keep your information in front of employees in many ways. Think about the lunch room or cafeteria in your facility and whether you can set out little table tents with various messages about compliance and privacy. If the organization writes a newsletter, you should have a "compliance corner" or some other regular spot to provide news and updates.

In large organizations, the marketing or communications person can be a huge asset when you establish a good working relationship. You can enlist this person's help to find creative ways to get your message out, such as organizing and promoting Compliance Week activities, which can be a great opportunity not only to raise awareness about compliance and privacy, but also to get to know employees. You can find lots of ideas for events on HCCA's website or on the sites of other organizations that focus on compliance. This is a good chance to think about the culture and size of your organization and which activities might get employees engaged. Contests are usually well received; for example, you can post questions in the newsletter or on the intranet site and do a drawing of correct answers for a prize. People always like to win a prize! You can set up a table in the lunch room with giveaways and information.

One thing to bear in mind is that other departments host "weeks" as well, so make sure you're not up against Nursing Week or something like that ... unless you can piggyback off of it to get more traction. Usually, the Communications department maintains a schedule of events, or the schedule may be on the intranet site, so check the calendar before you start planning.

The last area to discuss with respect to communication is one that I feel strongly about. Unless you work in a very small practice, the organization should have an intranet site with a general home page that appears when employees log on to their computers. The company intranet site is different from the organization's public *internet* site that patients and others can find online. The intranet site provides a list of departments or various tabs and topics that employees can click for information. Compliance and privacy needs to have its own page. I cannot overstate the importance of this in terms of communicating with employees. It's the only way you can really reach most employees, because it's not realistic to expect that you will be able to attend every department meeting or meet and greet all staff. If you have a good intranet site, however, you can keep updates available to employees, along with links to resources, policies, articles, and educational tools. In addition to the obvious efficiencies you gain, having an intranet site also demonstrates to the government, if you ever have to, that employees have access to compliance information.

You can cross-reference your newsletter and intranet site. For instance, if you run a contest, publish a teaser about it in the newsletter that sends people to the intranet site. Your intranet page can have an "Ask the Compliance Officer" button, which is another way to provide access to you. And, of course, post the hotline number front and center. Interconnect all of the various communication pieces to really engage people and keep their interest.

Employees really need to know about the intranet site for compliance, especially where to find the policies. If a regulator ever comes to visit, it is not unlikely that this person will ask employees to show how they access compliance and privacy policies. All employees should be able to answer that question. They should also, by the way, know who you are. Being known to employees is not too challenging in a small place; but in a large organization, especially one that is decentralized and has multiple locations, it can be easier said than done.

New employees who saw you at orientation will probably remember you, but others … not so much. One way to get a sense of where employees in your organization are is to go on a walkabout. Ask random employees what they would do if they had a compliance concern. Who would they call? See whether they know about the hotline. Ask them where the policies are. And, last, ask them who the compliance officer is. It's funny—but not really—when they name someone else or say there is none. You know then that you need to get yourself out there more and be visible in the organization.

# DISCIPLINARY STANDARDS

Disciplinary standards are important from a compliance perspective because employees who violate compliance or privacy requirements need to be disciplined, and disciplined in a consistent manner. This can be a challenge in a small organization, where everyone knows each other. In that situation, employees know the personal business of their colleagues, everyone has a story, and it's difficult to apply strict standards sometimes. That being said, treating employees differently without a rational reason can create legal liabilities for the organization, so developing and following standards are necessary.

In a large organization, the challenge is that different employees have different roles and different managers, and the applied standards may be vastly different. This can be an issue not only from a compliance enforcement perspective, but also from a Human Resources perspective. It creates a risk for the organization when similarly situated employees are not treated the same. And as I said earlier about communication, employees will talk, and word gets around. You don't want an employee in one location who does something wrong to get fired for it, and someone similar in another location to get no discipline or even a promotion! This can happen when employee discipline isn't monitored and standards are not well established. Consistency is key to demonstrate equality and fairness in discipline.

So, how do you manage this issue effectively, especially when discipline is generally handled between management and Human Resources? The standard to have in place is commonly referred to as a sanctions policy, but I like to refer to it informally as the "levels of badness" policy.

Typically, a sanctions policy sets out three different levels of violations, with examples. A first-level violation usually is an infraction that was not done intentionally and is not the result of someone trying to circumvent the rules. A middle-level issue is when an employee who knew better for some reason (other than for personal gain) ignored the standards in place. A third-level offense results from an employee violating the standards for personal gain or malice. For example, an employee sells patient information to an identity thief. Clearly, that is an entirely different issue from one in which an employee accidentally faxes a medical record to the wrong number.

These three levels are important because they distinguish between the intent and the harm caused in each situation. The sanctions system should also take into account mitigating and exacerbating circumstances, which may influence the discipline imposed. A mitigating circumstance lessens the charge, such as when an employee comes forward and offers information about an issue, even if he or she was a party to it. An exacerbating circumstance worsens the level of wrongdoing, such as when an employee's action in addition to violating the standard also causes significant harm to the organization, to an individual, or to both.

The sanctions policy, and disciplinary issues generally, is challenging to deal with because it is the domain of Human Resources. Most HR people will assert that the organization has a progressive disciplinary policy, thank you very much. So, this is another area in which you can provide education from a compliance perspective, because the issue is not about progressive discipline, but about the consistent handling of compliance violations.

The sanctions policy must work in conjunction with the progressive disciplinary standards HR has established. Once members of the HR department understand the three-level discipline concept, get them to partner with you in this activity and support it. I have witnessed approval and implementation of a sanctions policy held up two years—really!—by an HR leadership team that could not come to terms with collaborating on developing a unified system; and that kept coming back with different examples of what should be included or possibly wasn't addressed, therefore warranting another rewrite. A good sanctions policy includes examples of each level of violation, and everyone has an opinion about the examples and missteps that should or should not be included. Plus, the fact that Compliance is proposing a system that steps right into HR territory leads naturally to the inclination to resist. It is important that you build a strong relationship with HR so this process can function and flow smoothly.

Although HR and the executive team may understand the policy and the rationale behind it, when an incident arises, management may be loath to apply the standards to the employee in question. Some managers are strict, by the book; and others really want to consider the individual employee and the fact that the employee is a single mom or is taking care of a sick parent, or whatever circumstance has affected that employee. Human Resources may or may not buy in to that as well, so that's another dynamic to be prepared for.

Your challenge here is to come across as flexible, but it is important to be consistent and not allow excuses for every employee who violates the company's standards. I have found that if you listen and discuss with HR and management, it is possible to come up with a solution that you can live with but that is also as fair as can be, even if there are extenuating circumstances.

Sometimes, of course, there are simply no extenuating circumstances you can buy in to, given the level of infraction. In such instances, it's important to hold your ground. If employees get the idea that Compliance isn't taken seriously, then more incidents will likely follow. Like everything else we have discussed, delivering sanctions in a fair and comprehensive way can be a delicate balancing act. You want to establish trust and rapport and show employees that your role primarily is to support staff in the organization by acting as a resource. But you also want them to understand that you won't allow violations of laws, regulations, policies, or procedures, because your job is to protect the organization from risk. Your job is not to protect the employees. All of this is intended to help you find that balance. Employee discipline is an area that can be troublesome, particularly if you are a compassionate person; everyone has a story.

Another issue to be aware of is unions. Find out whether you are entering a union environment, because, if so, discipline all of a sudden becomes a much more complicated matter that involves a host of people, including leadership and the Legal department. Yikes. Even new policies relating to discipline need a whole other level of scrutiny. So, just beware of that wrinkle, should you need to.

# RISK ASSESSMENTS

Some people consider risk assessments to be another component of an effective compliance program; others consider it part of auditing and monitoring. In any event, you need to understand the rationale behind risk assessments and be prepared to engage in this activity either annually or, preferably, on an ongoing basis. In either case, you need to document risk assessments and show how you use the results.

A risk assessment is basically an evaluation of the organization's compliance risk. In the past, we conducted risk assessments by looking at the annual OIG Work Plan, pulling out the issues that potentially pertained to our organization, and surveying the organization's exposure for those issues.

Risk assessments have evolved right alongside compliance programs. In the past, compliance programs used to be all about making sure you were coding and billing correctly. Ah, the good ole days.

Now you have financial arrangements, quality indicators, medical necessity, meaningful use, HIPAA, and a whole bunch of other regulatory requirements and enforcement initiatives that bear little resemblance to the "old-style" compliance program.

Without getting too technical here, risk is assessed by multiplying likelihood by severity. Either of these factors can be high, medium, or low. So, a risk assessment ranks the potential risks in your organization. You can create your own variation of this model so long as it provides a meaningful way to evaluate risks and your leadership agrees with the methodology.

Potential risks present from multiple sources. You need to consider enforcement activity, OIG fraud alerts, hotline calls, the OIG Work Plan, new laws and regulations, any government audits or investigations you've had, and other types of issues that have come across your desk from a myriad of sources. Once you have identified your "parade of horribles," you must verify how much of a concern the issues may be. You can do this using a variety of mechanisms, and you may decide to alternate from year to year, just to ration out the intensity of resource use.

One popular method is to survey the department heads. Surveys have the advantage of being standardized and less time-consuming for you and for the recipients. You ask functions to rank their own risks, and then you have your data. The downside to this process is that the assessment of likelihood is subjective and inconsistent. It also might be biased by management, which is looking to avoid adding work or doesn't really understand what you are asking in the first place. Survey results sometimes are not accurate or useful.

Another strategy is to conduct interviews. In large organizations, interviewing is hugely resource-intensive. The benefit, however, is that you can drill down and explain the questions, ask for clarification, discuss potential risks, and obtain better information all while also providing education and building relationships.

You can combine the two: Start with a survey and then follow-up on specific issues you have questions about. That's not a bad approach and at least gives you some face time with managers and an opportunity to probe areas when necessary. I like this approach because it balances resource use with the ability to spend time exploring the areas of greatest potential risk.

In any event, risk assessments are an important component of what you do and will form the basis of your work planning. A risk assessment that doesn't lead to a work plan is a dangerous thing, because it shows that the organization knows where its problems are and doesn't care enough to take action. Most organizations expect to see a risk assessment paired with a work plan, even if they don't know much else about what you do.

The other type of risk assessment is an assessment of the compliance program itself. You should not conduct this evaluation, except when you first join the organization. It's fine to start your new job with an assessment; it's appropriate in order to figure out what to do first. If you are doing a program assessment, you need to survey the elements I have outlined here and determine what is missing, inadequate, or outdated. Then you can set up a plan for your first ninety days, six months, twelve months, and so on.

Once you're ensconced in the role, however, it is a good idea to obtain an outside review of the compliance program. Bringing in an outside consultant now and then to review your program is beneficial for two reasons. First, it shows objectivity. Second, it gives you a fresh perspective and perhaps some new ideas. It is easy to get used to doing things a certain way, no matter how well informed you keep yourself. An injection of fresh thinking from outside can help shake things up a bit, and that's not a bad thing; you should welcome such input. Plus, if you are having trouble with support or resources, an outside opinion can shine a light on where you need to invest additional effort and backs up concerns or requests you've made in the past, if any.

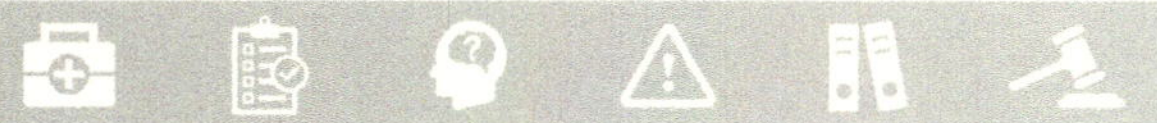

# PART II

# SPECIFIC CHALLENGES AND ISSUES

THE SECOND PART OF THIS handbook focuses on key issues that come up regularly for compliance officers. They require special attention and awareness, because they carry risks if handled incorrectly.

# GOVERNMENT AUDITS AND INVESTIGATIONS

As a compliance officer, you will be front and center for handling incoming government audits and investigations. Obviously, you hope neither will happen, but you need to be ready. Even if you think the organization has no issues, and you've been doing your job to monitor and audit your own facility, you might miss something or a previous problem can resurface.

First, identify where government audit notices come in the door of the organization. You may be surprised to find that there can be more than one entry place, depending on the size of your organization and the lines of business. This occurs because different government agencies have identified different in-house contact people and owners of the various types of records.

Think about all the organizations that can conduct audits. In addition to private payers, such as Blue Cross/ Blue Shield, other agencies work on behalf of Medicare. They change with some regularity, as well. There are Recovery Auditors (formerly known as Recovery Audit Contractors, or RACs), and Zone Program Integrity Contractors (ZPICs), and the actual Fiscal Intermediaries who administer the Medicare program. Medicare (CMS) also can do quality audits and audits to verify compliance with meaningful use and HIPAA. Because the Medicare program is so huge, with a variety of types of auditors, many contractors conduct reviews.

It can be confusing at first to get audit requests and really not understand who is auditing you. The letter sent should be explanatory, but if you are confused, check the CMS website or call the contractor to verify who they are and what program they work with. You must know this so that you can figure out which regulatory requirements they are looking at and which records they should have access to.

Medicaid also conducts audits, adding another potential set of reviews. Medicaid reviews happen at the state level, so implementation may vary from state to state. The Office of Civil Rights (OCR) also audits, including HIPAA audits, as do the Department of Justice, the Health and Human Services Office of Inspector General (OIG), and many others. Even the FBI reviews healthcare fraud cases on occasion.

Given all the potential audits, reviews, and investigations, it can be challenging to manage the load if you are in a large organization. Don't be surprised to learn that audit requests are being handled without you ever hearing a peep about them. It can take some time to get your arms around this, to develop a good process, and to educate all the departments about how audit requests should be managed.

Many organizations have allocated resources to a process for managing RAC audits (Recovery Audit Contractors, or Recovery Auditors, who are engaged by CMS). Find out about this, because if a solid process is set up for RAC audits, but other types of audits are decentralized, you have an opportunity to consolidate all the audits and to use one tool for tracking and reporting. Make this a priority, because in large companies, managing (or even monitoring) multiple routine and nonroutine audits and investigations can be extremely challenging.

It's important to be on top of auditing, because missing a deadline for producing records or meeting other deadlines can cost the organization a lot of money, in addition to potentially raising red flags with the auditing agency. From its perspective, lack of response to an audit letter can signify a problem or at least a lack of cooperation. Managing audit requests is critical.

Another good reason for keeping close track of reviews is so that as part of your ongoing risk assessment process, you can monitor the types of issues attracting the attention of government contractors and payers. The degree of formality you apply to this process is up to you and your organization; but if you see a trend in data requests, jump on top of it and conduct your own review and corrective action if necessary. Once the government or a payer spots some deviation or irregularity in your claims, the reviews will keep coming. You need to figure out what is going on and fix it.

The last reason for centralizing your audit and data requests is that you should report the activity to the Compliance Committee and, in summary fashion, to the board or board committee. You need to be able to explain which issues are being audited, by whom, and why. You need to be able to answer the question of what it's costing the organization and what you are doing to correct the problem. Audits and investigations cost money and can become bigger problems, so inform leadership about them and know what is going on at all times.

Once you have the actual process figured out, what do you actually do when you get an audit request?

First, read the request carefully to make sure you understand what it is asking for and what time frame applies. There are so many ways that audits are managed, and so many contractors, there is no single process. The most important factor is to follow the instructions in the letter. Some will inform you that the payer is denying a claim and that it's up to you to dispute that outcome. Others are postpay reviews, also known as "pay and chase" and are conducted retroactively. The auditor may or may not tell you why it is targeting this particular service.

It is standard practice to pull the requested records immediately to determine your risk before responding. This is particularly true if you aren't sure what is being audited. Pulling the claim and the documentation may quickly point to the problem.

In addition to determining the particular risk for this audit request, look at your database to see whether you've gotten similar requests in the recent past. If so, that's a pretty good indication of where you have some work to do.

If you find no similar audit requests, consider how deep to dig to see whether this claim or service is an isolated incident or part of a larger problem. That is really a judgment call to the extent that you may have a good reason to believe it is a one-time issue. I caution you, however, that it is better to do some form of review to uncover other instances.

Two factors relate to reviewing the issue, even if the error appears to be completely random or minimal. One, if the data show a pattern, you will keep getting audit requests on the issue. The government's perspective is that you are on notice when you get audit requests, so if you simply keep responding one by one, it gives the appearance that you aren't concerned about addressing the underlying issue and that you are waiting for them to ask for money or to not pay on a case by case basis. In other words, you don't really care that it isn't being done correctly. That isn't a good impression to create.

The other factor has to do with overpayments. If you get an audit request on claims that have already been paid, you are expected to exercise due diligence in identifying overpayments created by the issue and repaying them promptly.

CMS makes it clear in the recent Final Rule, published on February 12, 2016, that overpayments are expected to be reported and returned within sixty days of identification, which is the point when the overpayment is actually quantified. The rule also states, however, that reasonable diligence is required to identify overpayments, and that compliance measures should be in place to achieve that goal. This once again not only reaffirms the government's expectations about compliance programs, but also establishes a duty for organizations to proactively monitor for potential overpayments.

So, do your review and develop a corrective action plan if necessary. Repay overpayments promptly by following the process the applicable carriers or payers outline. In addition, if the issue was caused by a human error (as opposed to, for instance, a technology system problem) and the employees have been given training, be sure to verify that the behavior has been corrected.

The corrective action plan is significant in government audits and investigations, so having a solid template and process is critical. If the government becomes aware of a compliance issue in your organization, the best action you can take is to show that you have already developed a corrective action plan (don't wait for the government to tell you to do this), which you share. Be sure that you include the key points I have already mentioned: training or retraining employees, repaying overpayments, and reauditing the area. Include the other actions you take to rectify the situation, as well, such as revising policies, fixing technology systems, and so forth. The main idea here: Demonstrate to the government that you take compliance seriously and that you quickly moved to fix the problem.

When you work with the government, the best approach is to be cooperative and show that you want to work with it to resolve the issues. Most auditors I have met have been easy to work with, and if you talk to them, they can be very reasonable. Of course, if you are under investigation, that is a different issue; work closely with legal counsel to make sure you manage an investigation carefully. In either event, you need to be cooperative, which goes a long way in determining how the agency will treat you and the company.

The last issue I'd like to discuss with respect to audits and investigations is that the various government agencies do not necessarily coordinate or even have awareness of what their counterparts are doing, although they are supposed to. With that in mind, more than one agency might try to review the same issue or even the same claims. This is another reason to carefully track audit requests, audits, and past audits. If a claim has already been audited, the payer should not look at it again, especially if it already took the money back! Just be aware that overlaps like this can happen, and it is up to you to stay on top of it all.

Conversely, private payers and government agencies to some extent share information. In the past, government investigators partnered with private payers in workgroups (I was actually on one of these workgroups; other members included the FBI, state attorney generals, and fraud investigators from health and auto insurance companies). And at a recent conference, the OIG announced it was establishing a more collaborative approach with the private sector for fraud prevention and detection, so this model is currently being emphasized. This is relevant because, again, you need to know that private payers may also send you an audit request for their own claims relating to an issue the government is also interested in.

# FRAUD, WASTE, AND ABUSE

PREVENTING AND DETECTING fraud, waste, and abuse are the underlying purposes of compliance programs, so it makes sense to discuss what this entails. The terms refer to different types of activities, and I'll start with some clarification.

> *Fraud* is generally defined as knowingly and willfully executing, or attempting to execute, a scheme or artifice to defraud any healthcare benefit program or to obtain (by means of false or fraudulent pretenses representations, or promises) any of the money or property owned by, or under the custody or control of, any healthcare benefit program. (18 U.S.C. § 1347)
>
> *Waste* is overutilization of services or other practices that, directly or indirectly, result in unnecessary costs to the healthcare system,

including the Medicare and Medicaid programs. It is not generally considered to be caused by criminally negligent actions, but by the misuse of resources.

*Abuse* includes any action or actions that may, directly or indirectly, result in one or more of the following:

- Unnecessary costs to the healthcare system, including the Medicare and Medicaid programs
- Improper payment for services
- Payment for services that fail to meet professionally recognized standards of care
- Services that are medically unnecessary

Abuse involves payment for items or services when there is no legal entitlement to that payment, and the healthcare provider or supplier has not knowingly or intentionally misrepresented facts to obtain payment. It isn't always as straightforward to identify abuse as it is to distinguish fraud, and it requires a review of the facts and circumstances, including the intent of the parties.

In the beginning, when compliance programs were initially established in health care, the majority of compliance issues revolved around various coding and billing issues. This is clear both in the early

OIG *Compliance Program Guidance for Hospitals*, for instance, and in the perspectives of those who were developing programs in those early days.

The False Claims Act, which was (and still is) the tool most frequently used, dates all the way back to the days of President Lincoln and was intended to address issues of war profiteering. In 1986, President Reagan amended the FCA, which resulted in greater penalties and reinstated the *qui tam* provision that provided rewards for "whistleblowers."

The Health Insurance Portability and Accountability Act of 1996 (HIPAA) provided additional resources to address fraud and abuse, which by that time was becoming well recognized as a significant problem that cost government healthcare programs huge amounts of money.

Obviously, we know that claims that misstate services or supplies provided are fraudulent and violate the federal False Claims Act. The classic scenarios involved issues such as upcoding, where a provider bills for a higher level of services than was provided, or duplicate billing, where multiple bills are submitted in order to secure extra reimbursement for the same service. Another early issue had to do with teaching hospitals and how they used residents and billed for services. These reviews, conducted by the OIG in the 1990s, were referred to as Physicians at Teaching Hospitals, or PATH, audits. The OIG discovered that teaching physicians were not adequately documenting their involvement (and supervision) in patient care and were, in some cases, upcoding services as well.

The PATH audits were noteworthy because they represented a systematic and targeted review by the OIG that resulted in large-dollar payments. They were subsequently challenged on the terms of the OIG's authority to conduct such audits. The General Accounting Office (GAO) reviewed the appropriateness of the reviews and the methodology the OIG used. The GAO, in a July 1998 report, found that the reviews were within the HHS OIG's purview, and that the methodology was sound.

There was a recommendation, however, that the OIG focus on risk-based reviews rather than attempting to audit all teaching hospitals. The GAO noted that concerns with billings by teaching physicians had been ongoing for many years and reiterated the requirements for teaching physicians to either provide the services or supervise the resident who performed the service. The GAO also noted that the application of the False Claims Act was appropriate, rather than merely seeking repayments, and that this was effective as a deterrent to healthcare fraud and abuse.

This GAO opinion is significant not only for the specific issue related to teaching physicians, but also more broadly as an affirmation of the OIG's authority for conducting these types of audits and seeking settlements.

Although the OIG was tasked with investigating healthcare fraud and abuse at its inception in the 1970s, the PATH audits attracted the attention of people in health care because the size of the settlements was publicized; and people started to understand how a failure of compliance can really cost an organization, both in terms of money and reputation.

As the 1990s progressed, the purview and nature of fraud and abuse audits evolved beyond coding, billing, and typical False Claims Act cases. Audits started really digging into complex financial and referral arrangements.

The two laws that come into play here are the Anti-Kickback Statute and the Stark Law. The Anti-Kickback Statute makes it illegal to pay or receive remuneration for referrals; and the Stark Law, also known as the "physician self-referral statute," deals specifically with physicians who refer business to organizations where they have a financial interest.

One of the primary areas where enormous cases relating to the Anti-Kickback Statute have been settled is pharmaceuticals. These cases are so many variations on a theme: Basically, they involve pharmaceutical companies paying physicians or healthcare providers to use or promote their products. In addition to the kickback issue, many of the companies get in trouble for off-label marketing, when a drug is not approved for a specific use by the Food and Drug Administration, but the drug company promotes it for that use anyhow. In many cases, the pharmaceutical companies were paying physicians to promote their medications for off-label use, thus resulting in a kickback case and an off-label marketing case.

These cases have settled in amounts of hundreds of millions of dollars and have sparked a whole new area of focus for not only government investigations, but also compliance program activities. The pharmaceutical industry got into the game to mitigate the damage to their financials and to their reputations. Pharmaceutical Research and Manufacturers of America (PhRMA) developed guidance for the industry that outlines which activities are and are not acceptable. This is a very useful document, called the *Code on Interaction with Health Care Professionals*, which you should review and keep handy as a reference tool.

AdvaMed is an industry group that represents companies that develop and manufacture medical products, technologies, and services. AdvaMed created a similar guidance document for its own companies, titled *Code of Ethics on Interactions with Health Care Professionals*. The two documents are similar and are helpful for you to use as you develop your own policies and internally if you have a conflict that relates to one of these issues.

As a compliance officer, it is important to understand that you have a very definite role in monitoring these relationships. When we talk about vendor relations later, I provide practical examples of the types of activities that you should embark on with respect to vendors. The main point here is that any situation in which someone, whether a pharmaceutical or device manufacturer, a clinical laboratory, or some other person or individual who may make or receive referrals, is giving or receiving something of value, it needs to fit within specific guidelines. A kickback can come in many forms: tickets to a sporting event, a trip to a conference or other industry event, a lease for which the rate is not based on fair market value, or the provision of free services between providers.

When the huge pharmaceutical cases emerged, and the industry responded, many organizations tightened their policies. Some took a very conservative approach and banned gifts and meals altogether. Others, however, have deeply ingrained practices and cultures, and you will have a difficult time getting those physicians and others to say goodbye to their frequent attendance at sporting events and other goodies. One key message to convey when you are talking to physicians, leaders, and employees about kickback risks is to explain that under that law, both the party that gives and the party that receives may be found liable. Yes, the drug and device companies have taken a huge hit. But physicians have been prosecuted as well. The government has made it quite clear that it is looking for individual culpability when an organization gets in trouble, so people need to understand their risk if they engage in these behaviors.

The Stark Law is narrower than the Anti-Kickback Statute to the extent it applies only to physicians. There are a number of exceptions for different types of physician arrangements; but in order to get protection under an exception, the arrangement does need to be structured in accordance with the exception requirements. Close doesn't cut it.

Some of the more common exceptions to Stark include arrangements such as personal services, employment, and leases. Exception requirements under Stark are similar to those of the Anti-Kickback Statute: The arrangement must be set out in writing, and the terms need to be for fair market value, without respect to volume or value of referrals, and commercially reasonable. In other words, the arrangement should make sense even if there were no referrals flowing.

Stark is very complex, and it is important to have a good Stark attorney as a resource. Physician arrangements need to be reviewed by counsel. If the organization uses a standard agreement, such as for employment, counsel should review and approve the template.

In the past, many organizations self-disclosed identified "technical" Stark violations. These violations included arrangements such as expired contracts or contracts that neither party had actually signed.

Sometimes self-audits revealed that small payments were made to physicians and no contract whatsoever was in place. These types of violations usually resulted from sloppiness or lack of understanding, rather than any intent to pay for referrals. The problem, however, is that Stark is a strict liability statute. A strict liability statute is one where intent doesn't matter. That is why the organizations that discovered these seemingly minor issues had to disclose to the government.

There has been some recent relief, however. In the *2016 Medicare Physician Fee Schedule*, CMS added exceptions and provided clarification around the writing requirement. Previously, the arrangement had to be documented in writing and signed by both parties. In the latest guidance, CMS states that the arrangement doesn't need to be contained all in one document, that it can be in various contemporaneous documents that sufficiently outline the details of the arrangement. In addition, the signatures of both parties, though still required, do not have to be on the same document.

I think part of the reason for this change is to address the heavy volume of self-disclosures about agreements that really weren't the result of bad intentions, even though intent isn't at issue under Stark. CMS was undoubtedly spending too much time and resources on cases that were relatively innocuous when those resources could be better spent on actual bad actors.

We haven't yet seen how this change will play out when the government does do an audit. For that reason, I discourage organizations from easing up on contracting and formally documenting physician arrangements. If your company has already done a self-disclosure, now is the time to talk to your Stark attorney about how to proceed. There may be some latitude, given the recent changes, for providers who have minimal infractions.

One other law that you may or may not hear about is the Foreign Corrupt Practices Act (FCPA). I'm not going to dive into this law except to let you know that it pertains to the bribery of foreign public officials. So, unless you work for an international organization, it probably won't ever come up. Large pharmaceutical and device manufacturers that sell their products or do research overseas are affected the most. Foreign government-owned hospitals become subject to the FCPA, because those in the organization are considered "foreign officials" under the law. If you have a position in an organization that does business internationally, learn more about FCPA.

One general suggestion related to fraud and abuse: Discourage employees from using the "F word" (fraud), particularly in emails, when they think they have identified a problem. Employees can be prone to drama, and there are always certain people who love to send a message to the compliance officer, CFO, and others, stating that they have done a routine department review and identified fraud. Yikes. Even worse is if they take it upon themselves to estimate an amount of "overpayment." This does happen, I have seen it; and then you get an entire executive team in a tailspin over an issue that may or may not even be an overpayment, much less fraud.

But if that word is used in an email message and there ever is a lawsuit or government investigation, that message will be discoverable and can cause all sorts of trouble. Part of your job is to help employees understand that if they find something they think is a problem, they need to *talk* to their leader, or to you, before moving forward on their own and certainly before broadcasting the F word over email. I can't emphasize this enough. I have seen it too many times, and it always makes my hair stand on end. Employees also need to understand that errors are not the same thing as fraud.

Consider the situation from this perspective: The employee who sends that email may believe fraud is going on (the employee's understanding of what fraud actually is may be completely erroneous), and the message gets everyone in an uproar. You do an audit and discover what the problem is, and it really isn't nearly what the employee thought. You resolve it, or so you believe, but then suddenly you get a request from the government. The employee doesn't think you handled the issue—maybe they believe you swept it under the rug—so reported it. Perhaps the employee also alleges retaliation, too. Now you have legal expenses and a government investigation, even if there was no fraud from the start. It can happen. Even if, at the end of the day, you are cleared of wrongdoing, you will have spent an inordinate amount of time and resources managing the issue.

Also, once the government starts auditing your records, you never know what it may find that you didn't know about; so another issue may appear that causes a prolonged review. Nobody is perfect, and good auditors can usually find something if they look hard enough. I'm not suggesting you are trying to put one over on the government; I'm just saying that it is far better to handle issues internally in an appropriate way. It is more economical and efficient for the organization, and it certainly saves a lot of drama. My point is that you need to educate your people.

# ETHICS AND COMPLIANCE

THE TERMS *ETHICS* AND *compliance* are sometimes used interchangeably because their meaning is misunderstood. *Ethics* refers to the organization's guiding principles and values. *Compliance* refers to adherence to laws, rules, regulations, and organizational policies. You can think of this as the difference between morality and law, which is a roughly comparable analogy.

Different organizations have different perspectives on ethics and cultures that support that view. Although you are unlikely to find an organization that claims to be committed to unethical behavior, you may find yourself in an organization that really believes the entire purpose of a compliance program is to keep people out of jail. In these organizations, the compliance plan (if one exists) defines the compliance program mission as adhering to laws and regulations.

At the other end of the spectrum, you will find organizations that include *ethics* or *integrity* in either the department title or your title. For example, "compliance and ethics officer" or "chief integrity officer." Now, of course, saying it doesn't make it so, but it does demonstrate an intent and awareness that are probably not evident in the other kinds of organizations.

Do titles matter? My opinion is that they do, so long as the culture and behavior of leadership are consistent with the intent behind a title. Like many other issues I discuss in this book, I have seen that go both ways.

The role of ethics in health care is an interesting one. To put it simply, there are two different types of ethics in health care, which is why you might be confused if your role includes ethics.

*Medical ethics* deals with those moral choices related to actual health care, such as end-of-life decision making. These are obviously complex and sensitive issues and are not typically within the domain of a compliance officer.

*Business ethics*, on the other hand, deals with questions of right or wrong in business dealings. These ethical questions are largely not unique to health care, except to the extent that they involve issues like paying for referrals (kickbacks) and similar healthcare-related scenarios.

In explaining the distinction, I refer to the Karen Ann Quinlan case as a medical ethics case versus

Enron, which was a well-known business ethics (and legal) case. If you are employed in an organization that expects you to have a role in business ethics, it is a good idea to be able to explain these differences, because people often confuse them.

Entire books are written on and multiple dedicated experts devote their time, energy, and expertise to issues involving business ethics. Many people who incorporate ethics into compliance training explain ethics as "doing the right thing when nobody is watching." Although that is clearly simplistic, it does serve to distinguish conceiving of compliance as a "don't get caught" issue versus a "do the right thing" culture. My preference is to work on instilling, or supporting, a culture based on an ethical framework, and my hope for you is that you are associated with such an organization or can move the culture in that direction.

# SELF-DISCLOSURES

THE TERM *SELF-DISCLOSURE* frequently refers to when an organization self-reports a compliance issue to the government. This simple definition can be confusing, however, because the OIG wrote an actual Self-Disclosure Protocol (SDP) and a similar process for Stark-only disclosures for CMS. The CMS process is called the Self-Referral Disclosure Protocol (SRDP) and is intended to facilitate the resolution of matters that, in the disclosing party's reasonable assessment, are actual or potential violations of the physician self-referral law (i.e., Stark). This requirement can be found under 6409(a) of the Affordable Care Act (ACA).

The OIG Self-Disclosure Protocol provides a tool and process for providers to proactively self-disclose instances of fraud and abuse to the government. The protocol was originally developed in 1998 and has been updated since that time, with the most recent update in 2013. The purpose of the process is to allow providers to disclose and resolve identified issues, rather than undergo a government audit or investigation with a resulting settlement. The OIG's position is that it is in the provider's best interest to self-disclose and that the government will view organizations that self-disclose more favorably. There is no specific promise of reduced penalties, although the OIG does claim generally that self-reporting mitigates fines and other penalties and usually prevents the imposition of a Corporate Integrity Agreement (CIA). The repayment of overpayments, also, is suspended during the pendency of the CIA.

The SDP is not intended to be used for every type of self-disclosure or for obtaining an OIG opinion. Issues strictly involving billing or overpayment errors that are not violations of laws are not suitable for the SDP, nor are Stark-only violations (which are handled through the CMS process referenced above). The SDP is intended to resolve violations of criminal, civil, or administrative laws that are subject to civil monetary penalties. Stark Law violations that are accompanied by a violation of the Anti-Kickback Statute are eligible for disclosure under the SDP. A variety of specific requirements relate to both types of disclosures, and you can find all the pertinent details on the OIG and CMS websites.

At the time of filing the SDP, the provider needs to state that the issue being disclosed is a potential violation of a specific law. The disclosing party needs to explain which law is potentially being violated, that the conduct has been stopped, and that corrective measures were put in place. It is generally true that anytime you advise a government agency about errors or compliance violations, you should be able to explain the scope of the issue and what actions you have taken to eliminate future occurrences. Don't even think of filing an SDP, however, without involving legal counsel.

If you discover that you have employed or contracted with an excluded person or organization, that issue is also subject to the SDP. Note that these disclosures are different from those for identified overpayments. Under Section 6402 of the ACA (42 U.S.C. § 1320a-7k[d]), providers may be found liable if they "fail to disclose and refund Medicare or Medicaid overpayments within the later of 60 days after the date the overpayment is identified or the date the next applicable cost report is due." Specifically:

> Section 6402 requires any person who has received an overpayment under Medicare or Medicaid to:
>
> (a) Report and return the overpayment to the Secretary, the State, or intermediary, a carrier or a contractor, as appropriate, at the correct address; and
>
> (b) Notify the Secretary, the State, intermediary, carrier or contractor to

> whom the overpayment was returned in writing of the reason for the overpayment.

This is a different type of disclosure and is not subject to the same process. For routine disclosures, although you still need to repay within sixty days of identification, you follow the process outlined by the fiscal intermediary or carrier. The carrier's website will include that information, or you can call and coordinate your repayment process. It is important to keep in mind that a failure to repay an identified overpayment may result in False Claims Act liability, which includes penalties up to $11,000 and treble damages.

The bottom line here is that you will use various processes for self-disclosure, depending on the facts and circumstances. If you discover a systematic error that affects government health program claims, your first conversation should be with legal counsel, who will guide you on the appropriate process. At that point you want direction in terms of attorney-client privilege, audit methodology, and reporting requirements. Legal counsel is invaluable to prevent any missteps that can make the problem worse.

Self-disclosure is obviously an area that can be confusing, even to people who deal with it all the time, because of the array of reporting requirements and processes. Gain an understanding of the various requirements in this subject area and keep an eye on developments, because they change from time to time.

### *The Yates Memo*

Another (somewhat) recent development, as of September 2015, was a memorandum issued by Assistant Attorney General Sally Yates. The purpose of the memo is to provide guidance to government attorneys regarding the prosecution of individuals. Historically, when an organization was found guilty of wrongdoing, fines and penalties were issued against the organization, but frequently no individuals were prosecuted. The Yates Memo is significant because it advises civil and criminal attorneys to work together to pursue individuals who are culpable in corporate malfeasance. Organizations will not be given credit for cooperation unless they produce a culpable individual.

Although government attorneys claim that this has always been their approach, never has a specific mandate on individual liability been identified and addressed. Corporate settlements are not to be entered into without at least a plan for dealing with the individuals involved, and the individual's ability to pay is irrelevant to the case. They will be pursued regardless.

What does this mean to the average organization? The obvious impact is that individuals are no longer able to hide behind the organization. It also means that organizations need to conduct internal investigations with the intention to identify individuals who had a role in the problem.

In reality, this may create an incentive for C-suite individuals to point the finger at lower-level employees in order to protect themselves. It's hard to say what actual impact this memo will have, but it could change how organizations conduct internal reviews.

As a compliance officer, you can do a couple of things. First, familiarize yourself with the Yates Memo and the previous guidance documents to fully educate your leadership. The board, the C-suite, and management should all understand this new landscape.

Second, review your internal investigation process. In a government audit or investigation, the government is looking for individual culpability. It will serve your organization well to have a rigorous investigation process in place and to show the government that you are fully cooperating.

### *Penalties and Consequences*

So, what are the typical risks to the organization in fraud and abuse issues? There are a variety of ways these situations can play out, and a lot depends on how cooperative the company is.

Fines and penalties are, of course, a standard outcome. To give you a sense of the magnitude of the arena, in 2015 the OIG recouped $2.4 billion for government healthcare programs and opened 983 new criminal healthcare fraud cases.

Although the fines and penalties can be dramatic, it is a mistake to think that the organization's costs end there; other consequences may be worse. One of the worst outcomes is to be excluded from participation in government programs. Once a provider or organization is excluded, other organizations that accept government health plans are no longer able to do business with or accept orders from the excluded entity. Excluded providers are on the OIG's List of Excluded Individuals and Entities (LEIE), for whatever period of time is decided, and that makes doing business difficult.

Another possible consequence for organizations violating fraud and abuse laws is the imposition of a Corporate Integrity Agreement (CIA). A CIA is an agreement between the provider and the government that enables the provider to avoid exclusion by agreeing to a variety of conditions. CIAs typically last three or five years. The requirements under a CIA vary depending on the facts and circumstances, but invariably include requirements relating to a compliance program, education, excluded provider checking and reporting, and specific audits and reviews to be conducted and reported routinely.

The CIA also requires that the organization hire an independent review organization (IRO). The IRO will audit the organization annually to ensure it meets the terms of the CIA, but you have to pay the IRO for this service. So, to save costs, you can do your own review, prepare your own report, and then hire the IRO to review it and any issues it deems appropriate or necessary. That depends on your level of confidence and the resources you have to do that work. Many organizations bring in a consulting or law firm to help with that, especially in the beginning.

CIAs can be burdensome for organizations, both in terms of costs and resources. First, there are the fines. Then, hiring an IRO is expensive, as is any law or consulting firm. And if you want to have attorneys advising you and possibly additional consultants to help you meet all the terms of the CIA, the costs really escalate.

Depending on what you already have implemented, it can be a fire drill trying to meet the CIA requirements and set up a full-blown compliance program. You will have to hire additional vendors and purchase systems (if you don't already have them) for the hotline and Lists of Excluded Individuals and Entities (LEIE) checking. Education and training requirements under a CIA are also extensive; they will vary, depending on the issues your organization had trouble with, but usually include general training as well as role-based training to address the organization's specific risk areas. A list of typical provisions follows. Note that they include key elements of an effective compliance program, as defined by the OIG:

- Hire a compliance officer and establish a Compliance Committee
- Develop and implement written standards and policies
- Develop and implement a comprehensive employee training program
- Establish and maintain a confidential disclosure program
- Eliminate any employment of, or contracting with, "ineligible persons," that is, individuals who have been excluded from participation in federal healthcare programs
- Specific reporting requirements, including overpayments, identified key events, and ongoing investigations and legal proceedings
- Repayment of overpayments in a timely manner
- Submission of an implementation report and annual reports to the OIG on the status of its compliance with the CIA requirements
- Retention of an independent review organization (IRO) to provide reviews of the specific risk areas defined in the CIA, including

issues such as arrangements, claims, transactions, and expenditures reviews

The main point to understand, and to help your leadership understand, is that a potential fine is not the total cost of a compliance violation. Say, for instance, your organization is subject to a CIA, and the fines are $2 million. That's bad, very bad. But it does not end there. You need to comply with the CIA or you will end up not only out the $2 million, but also as an excluded provider. So, after you pay the fine, and everyone is in a panic, you will need to hire an IRO. And you certainly want a good law firm with expertise in handling these matters. You may also want a compliance consultant to help you with the actual implementation of various policies, procedures, and training, particularly if you are building a new program. That $2 million can become $5 million, and that's in the first year. The organization is probably under a five-year CIA, so some of those costs will recur each year. The takeaway here is that the fine is not the end of the story.

In the meantime, the CIA is made public. A press release is generated and your agreement is published on the OIG website. Be sure to explain this issue to your leadership; nobody wants their business to have that kind of publicity. Depending on how large the organization is, how big a player it is in the market, and the size of the actual community, your disgrace can also hit the news. Though many organizations are under CIAs, if your organization is a big fish, the CIA will be newsworthy, so let's talk about the court of public opinion.

Various aphorisms remind us not to do things we wouldn't want published on the front page. This is particularly true for compliance issues because, if and when they become public, the organization will invariably appear to be greedy, immoral, deceitful, or some combination of those attributes. Think about public perception and the headlines dedicated to companies that get in trouble. It's easy to see how these issues can be publicized to paint a healthcare organization in a bad light:

- A hospital *bribes* physicians to send patients to it by sending the medical providers on trips and paying them unjustified bonuses.
- A health system *violates* patient trust by failing to implement privacy measures, and thousands of patient records are exposed.
- A laboratory or radiology company *devises* bogus lease arrangements with a local hospital to enhance Medicare referrals and payments.

The odds are stacked against providers and healthcare organizations that have committed transgressions (and I am not defending any bad behavior, believe me). Government players have plenty of motivation to publicize their settlements and recoveries. You can't blame them for this because they are recovering money that the government and taxpayers paid inappropriately, so that's not wrong in any way. They need to show that they are doing their job, and rightly so. Additionally, the media is motivated to share the scandal of the day or (stated more favorably) inform the public.

These are not insignificant issues from a business perspective. Healthcare providers have a trust relationship with their patients, so being called out publicly in such a way can be huge in terms of reputational damage. The thing is, although the organization may not have intentionally committed the infraction, it is perceived as a moral failing. Once it hits the local paper, it is nearly impossible to defend or deny the issue. So, the lesson here is to not let it happen, to put controls in place that minimize the likelihood of such an incident. You can never guarantee that nothing bad will happen, but you can compare the cost of your salary and your budget with some of the recent settlements and make a clear case that compliance is, indeed, a modest but valuable investment.

Here, it is imperative to point out that the run-on costs of lawyers, consultants, and expenses associated with a CIA that we discussed earlier are not limited to CIA-related events. In fact, they are not limited to fraud and abuse issues.

One of the biggest risks that can run up an organization's bill is a privacy or security breach. Think about all the notifications necessary: the process of going through an intensive risk assessment, the provision of credit monitoring services if identity theft is a risk, and the potential lawsuits from patients. On top of government fines and penalties. You can have a $10,000 penalty, and the public will think you got off easy; but what they don't realize is that the whole incident probably cost more like $10 million. Seriously. So, when you talk to leadership about the potential consequences of not investing in compliance, be armed with statistics or a list of the types of expenses that occur without good protections in place.

The government cares about whether an organization has an effective compliance program set up and is willing to invest in it. Compliance is not just a feel-good thing; it can save real money. First, as I explained earlier in the discussion of the Yates Memo, there is the issue of cooperation with an investigation. Cooperation credit can mean reduced penalties under the government's self-disclosure processes. Examples abound of organizations that failed to make an adequate effort at cooperation, and it cost them. Cignet Health Center, for instance, settled with the government for $4.3 million in a privacy case. Cignet was not allowing patients access to their records, but also did not cooperate with the Office of Civil Rights (OCR). That really wasn't very helpful to their case, adding $3 million to the total.

The takeaway should be clear: The cost of noncompliance can be vastly greater than the cost of supporting an effective compliance program. In addition, being a good corporate citizen can only help an organization in the eyes of the government and in the court of public opinion.

# OVERPAYMENTS

I HAVE ALREADY MENTIONED overpayments, so you may recall that, under the Affordable Care Act (ACA), it is a potential violation of the False Claims Act to retain identified overpayments. You might also hear this referred to as the "Reverse False Claims" statute.

The question of what it means to *identify* an overpayment has caused some consternation since the enactment of the ACA, but CMS clarified the definition in the *Federal Register* on February 12, 2016. According to CMS, a claim is identified once it's been quantified; in other words, once specific claims or amounts have been discerned or calculated. This is good news, especially because a New York court had ruled that a claim was identified once the *issue* was identified; that is, before an actual investigation and validation had occurred. That interpretation was alarming, given how much time it typically takes to complete a full investigation or audit, and then go through the repayment process.

The other relevant information in this recent *Federal Register* notice was that organizations do have a duty to exercise reasonable diligence once a potential overpayment situation is identified. Here, as in other guidance and regulations from various government bodies, it is clear that an effective compliance program is expected, including those processes that allow for the timely identification of potential overpayments. Not only are organizations expected to have processes in place, but they also need to act on any indication of potential overpayments to verify and identify those overpayments within six months.

This requirement is reasonable, in my opinion, and in some ways helpful to the compliance officer who received a hotline call or other tip about an issue, and the organization is delaying an actual audit to verify and quantify the amounts. I'm not suggesting that organizations are dishonest; but if no time frame is delineated for conducting such an audit, it is more likely to get pushed back, particularly if the facility is short on resources or has other pressing business. A compliance officer can find it necessary to pester to get the necessary resources, especially outside resources, for a review. The six-month time frame is actually not a bad thing; it keeps everyone honest and accountable.

The issue of overpayments is one that, as a compliance officer, you want to make key stakeholders understand thoroughly. For that reason, pull the February 12,

2016, issue of the *Federal Register* and other needed materials to prepare to educate employees and leaders and help resolve process-related questions.

An area you need to consider relates to credit balances. Credit balances are those amounts that the organization has been overpaid, often the result of multiple coverages, errors in patient-paid amounts, and other issues that are routine parts of business.

Medicare has very specific requirements on the identification, reporting, and repayment of credit balances: Credit balances must be reported and repaid on a quarterly basis. You can see why this may create a question: Overpayments must be repaid within sixty days of identification, and yet credit balances, by definition overpayments, need only be paid back quarterly.

To my knowledge, the courts have not weighed in to say that Medicare overpayments identified during the credit balance process should be handled differently from how they have been in the past. They are reconciled as part of a well-defined process required by CMS. Some organizations, in an abundance of caution, do pull out the Medicare overpayments and process them on a more frequent basis, however.

At this point, I believe that so long as credit balances are being managed appropriately, you are not incurring a risk related to "reverse false claims"; however, I am not giving legal advice on this question, particularly because things can change with one court case or OIG guidance document. One practical reason why this might be so is that the government, like everyone else, is trying to manage a heavy workload with fewer resources than it would like. It makes sense that it focuses its efforts on providers who appear to be truly violating laws and regulations—that's just my opinion. Mainly, be aware of the two repayment time frames and verify that your organization is reporting and repaying credit balances appropriately.

What else do you need to know about overpayments? A smart move is to figure out the causes of overpayments, beyond deliberate bad behavior related to documentation, billing, and coding. Errors can creep into the process in various places, beginning with patient registration. Inaccurate payer information in the system can result in overpayments or duplicate payments. Overpayments can result from confusion over what is billable under Part A and Part B, and which services are included in "bundled" charges. These are just a few obvious examples. You can see that overpayments don't all stem from one source, and there can be a full range of contributing factors: systems, processes, human errors, and (hopefully not) deliberate manipulation of information to increase revenue.

For information on how to handle routine overpayments due to government health programs, you can find the process online at the appropriate contractor's or agency's website. You can also talk to someone there if you have a procedural question. It's a good idea to develop a relationship with employees at those agencies. They will be easier to work with and will view your organization more favorably if they know you and see that you are being proactive.

One question that comes up routinely is how far back you need to go when you find a systemic overpayment problem. The February 2016 *Federal Register* did specify that there is a six-year lookback. This may seem onerous, but the proposed rule includes a ten-year lookback period. You may not need to go back even six years, however. Each situation is very fact-specific, and it really is determined by the cause of the problem. If, for instance, you changed a process two years earlier and that is when the problem started, you don't need to go back past that time. The main idea is to be able to state what caused the problem, demonstrate what you have done to correct it, and provide a timely repayment.

If the nature of the overpayment appears in any way suspicious, talk to legal counsel before going any further. Do the same if the issue is brought to your attention by Internal Audit or a department head who discovers a potentially significant or systematic error. You need to understand the nature of the issue and dig far enough into it to validate a likely problem, but talk to counsel before moving ahead. Don't do a full audit and then call the attorney, because he or she may advise you about issues such as attorney-client privilege, sampling and extrapolation, and other strategic and legal tips.

Another question that comes up regularly is about overpayments due to private payers and patients. If you have money that doesn't belong to you, you should return it, right? Private payers have contracts with providers, and those contracts should include requirements related to overpayments; adhere to the contract terms. And don't forget about state health plans, either; those are government health programs. With respect to patients, I recommend that you do not keep their money. That looks very bad if it lands on the front page of the local newspaper; plus, it just isn't right.

All that being said, if there are no legal or contractual obligations for certain types of overpayments, it makes sense to institute a threshold amount below which you won't chase down the owner and repay the amount. There is no universal number that I am aware of, but it's something you can discuss with the business office. Look at how much it actually costs to process a repayment, and then identify a threshold amount that seems reasonable. Make sure, however, you have a well-documented policy and procedure in place. This is not an area where you want it to appear the organization makes arbitrary decisions.

Last, be aware that organizations do not get to keep unclaimed overpayments. States have escheat laws that require reporting and payment to the state of unclaimed funds. Your finance people should be on top of this, as should you. Make sure that they know about this and are following the applicable laws.

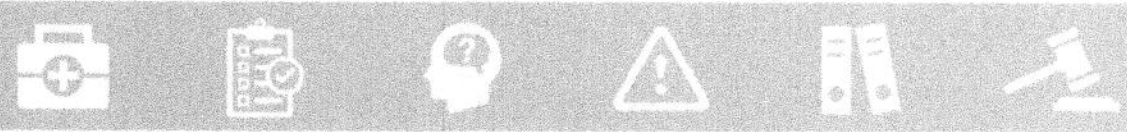

# VENDORS

A VAST ARRAY OF COMPLIANCE-RELATED concerns related to vendors can arise. If you review the various high-dollar settlements for healthcare fraud, many of the largest cases involve arrangements with pharmaceutical companies. For this reason, you need to treat vendor-related risk areas as high priority, including providing education to individuals in your organization who could be affected.

## *Gifts*

As you are probably aware, the OIG takes a very strict position regarding healthcare providers accepting gifts from vendors. These include meals and, particularly, more extravagant gifts such as trips, golf outings, and sports and entertainment tickets. Historically, giving these gifts was a common business practice among pharmaceutical and device representatives and physicians and others in a position to purchase or prescribe. They became accustomed to this way of doing business.

Things began to change when some of the big multimillion-dollar pharmaceutical cases were prosecuted, such as the TAP Pharmaceutical case in 2001 that settled for $875 million, the GlaxoSmithKline $3 billion settlement in 2012, and many others in between. A big driver in many of these cases had to do with off-label marketing practices coupled with paying kickbacks to physicians to help promote these off-label uses of the products.

In some of these cases, you can read discussions about the specific incriminating practices, including gifts paid to incentivize prescribing practices. The list of pharmaceutical companies prosecuted includes most, if not all, of the big names, and these huge cases shook the industry. As a result, Pharmaceutical Research and Manufacturers of America drafted a guidance document for the industry on the types of gifts that are and are not acceptable in order to curb the rising tide of settlements and fines.[1]

For example, the guidance discusses meals:

> In connection with such presentations or discussions, it is appropriate for occasional meals to be offered as a business courtesy to the healthcare professionals as well as members of their staff

[1] Code on Interactions with Healthcare Professionals, http://www.phrma.org/codes-and-guidelines/code-on-interactions-with-health-care-professionals.

> attending presentations, so long as the presentations provide scientific or educational value and the meals:
>
> (a) are modest as judged by local standards;
>
> (b) are not part of an entertainment or recreational event; and
>
> (c) are provided in a manner conducive to informational communication.

You can see, based on this example, that the culture and expectations around pharmaceutical vendors changed drastically. The other big area for change had to do with entertainment, as I mentioned earlier:

> To ensure the appropriate focus on education and informational exchange and to avoid the appearance of impropriety, companies should not provide any entertainment or recreational items, such as tickets to the theater or sporting events, sporting equipment, or leisure or vacation trips, to any healthcare professional who is not a salaried employee of the company. Such entertainment or recreational benefits should not be offered, regardless of:
>
> 1. the value of the items;
> 2. whether the company engages the healthcare professional as a speaker or consultant, or

3. whether the entertainment or recreation is secondary to an educational purpose.

This guidance document also addresses financial arrangements with physicians. In the past, and as noted in various OIG and Department of Justice (DOJ) documents regarding these cases, it was a common practice to pay physicians for marketing under the umbrella of "research." These activities might include surveys, speaking arrangements, or even paying the physicians to allow pharmaceutical reps to "shadow" them. The goal, of course, was to encourage the physicians to promote and prescribe the company's products. The OIG considered these activities "sham arrangements," and they played a large role in the cases where kickbacks were alleged. In the PhRMA guidance:

> Consulting Arrangements with healthcare professionals allow companies to obtain information or advice from medical experts on such topics as the marketplace, products, therapeutic areas, and the needs of patients. Companies use this advice to inform their efforts to ensure that the medicines they produce and market are meeting the needs of patients. Decisions regarding the selection or retention of healthcare professionals as consultants should be made based on defined criteria such as general medical expertise and reputation, or knowledge and experience regarding a particular

therapeutic area. Companies should continue to ensure that consultant arrangements are neither inducements nor rewards for prescribing or recommending a particular medicine or course of treatment. It is appropriate for consultants who provide advisory services to be offered reasonable compensation for those services and reimbursement for reasonable travel, lodging, and meal expenses incurred as part of providing those services. Any compensation or reimbursement made in conjunction with a consulting arrangement should be reasonable and based on fair market value. Token consulting or advisory arrangements should not be used to justify compensating healthcare professionals for their time or their travel, lodging, and other out-of-pocket expenses. The following factors support the existence of a bona fide consulting arrangement (not all factors may be relevant to any particular arrangement):

- a written contract specifies the nature of the consulting services to be provided and the basis for payment of those services;
- a legitimate need for the consulting services has been clearly identified in advance of requesting the services and entering into arrangements with the prospective consultants;

- the criteria for selecting consultants are directly related to the identified purpose and the persons responsible for selecting the consultants have the expertise necessary to evaluate whether the particular healthcare professionals meet those criteria;
- the number of healthcare professionals retained is not greater than the number reasonably necessary to achieve the identified purpose;
- the retaining company maintains records concerning and makes appropriate use of the services provided by consultants;
- the venue and circumstances of any meeting with consultants are conducive to the consulting services and activities related to the services are the primary focus of the meeting; specifically, resorts are not appropriate venues.

I share these specific sections from the PhRMA guidance because you may find the information useful in terms of developing your own standards and education around these issues. Organizations vary greatly in terms of their awareness and acceptance of the standards above, but these guidelines originate from the specific cases where healthcare providers and pharmaceutical companies got into expensive trouble with the government. For that reason, I recommend familiarizing yourself with these and the other standards included in the PhRMA guidance. I have always found it to be very helpful in terms of defining criteria for vendor arrangements, gifts, and meals.

As I've mentioned, some hospitals and providers have adopted a "no meals or gifts" policy, which certainly makes things much simpler. Others, however, are still routinely attending vendor-sponsored sporting events and sitting in the box seats nearly every week, despite the risk. Keep in mind that I am not talking about free samples here—samples are fine, so long as nobody bills for them. I am talking about actual gifts that benefit a healthcare professional who could potentially be influenced by those gifts.

Meals and gifts used to be an issue that was problematic to ferret out, unless recipients of goodies were inclined to disclose them on their annual conflict of interest disclosure (assuming, of course, one is in place). But now there is much more transparency around gifts and other remuneration that physicians and teaching hospitals receive from drug and device manufacturers.

Under the Physician Payments Sunshine Act, pharmaceutical and device manufacturers are required to disclose to CMS any payments made to physicians and teaching hospitals. These disclosures are made public by CMS in the Open Payments database (located on the CMS website). The physicians and teaching hospitals do have the option of registering and reviewing their information before it becomes public, but any disputes or disagreements are between them and the disclosing organization, not CMS. There is a great deal of variability in terms of who is aware of this database and how much they concern themselves with it. You may find some physicians who are registered and pay close attention, and others have no idea that such a thing exists.

The Open Payments database provides good insight into the physicians who work for an organization and into the hospital, if it is a teaching facility. You can use it in conjunction with an annual conflict of interest disclosure process to identify who is getting paid by industry and who is not being completely forthright on the internal disclosures.

The main advice I can provide regarding how to actually handle all of this is to tread lightly until you understand the lay of the land. It is critical to really grasp how the organization has viewed these arrangements in the past, how it perceives them now, and how well it understands these industry standards and issues. If you are entering an organization that has absolutely no idea of the risk and is still doing business the old-school way, you can make enemies very quickly by coming down hard and fast with all the rules.

I am not, in any way, recommending that you don't adopt appropriate standards. What I am saying is that relationships and credibility are important for you as you start out, so it is best to listen and learn before you start telling people how they need to fundamentally change the way they operate. Pick your battles and take your time, because this one is very sensitive. Find out the reason for that sensitivity, too, because it isn't just that physicians and hospitals are being greedy (some of them might be, but nonetheless, you have to work with them).

For instance, if you tell physicians that they cannot accept gifts because these are basically bribes to prescribe a certain medication, they will be outraged that you actually dare to suggest that a coffee mug or pizza could affect patient care decisions. Despite the fact that a variety of studies have shown that even a pen (yes, a pen) can influence behavior, the implication is offensive to physicians. Their indignation is not unreasonable, either, because any influence is not realized at a conscious level; the reason gifts and meals are so effective. Physicians don't actually think, ah, a pen was given, so I should prescribe this medication. It happens much more subconsciously, and it is insidious, kind of a quid pro quo but without awareness in most cases.

This is why I advise you to be sensitive and aware before pouncing on this issue; it definitely suggests you are questioning not only their integrity, but also their medical decision making by saying they can be bought with a pizza. Try to understand their position, and you will be better able to manage this issue in a way that doesn't offend.

### *Sponsorships*

Other gifts from vendors come in the form of sponsorships. Vendors may sponsor an educational session for physicians, may provide funding for your organization when they host an event, or may sponsor various fundraising activities that your company is promoting or supporting.

Sponsorships are tricky, because they do provide a real benefit to the organization or its patients. If you work for a nonprofit or charitable organization, for instance, of course you want all the donors you can get for your various fundraising activities and events. And, let's face it, the vendors often have deep pockets to promote goodwill with their customers or potential customers.

The key to sponsorships is separating the donation from the actual person or department with purchasing or prescribing authority. Let me give an example to help clarify. Say, for instance, you work for a large nonprofit health system. Your Home Services division is actively raising money and is hosting an annual fundraiser. This line of business deals a lot with a durable medical equipment (DME) supplier, which is happy to spend a lot of money to buy a table at your organization's event. Can you accept it?

You may think no, because it would influence the Home Services group, but in actuality it can be done. The correct course is to route all fundraising through the foundation or fundraising department. This means that the Home Services manager who actually deals with the DME company should *not* be calling it about the event. Someone from the foundation should. Likewise, if the DME company writes a check, it should not hand it to its usual point of contact; the check should go to the foundation.

Implementing this process can be challenging operationally, because relationships between vendors and the organization exist at the department or function level, so leaders in those divisions will want to reach out to vendors. On the basis of their relationship, after all, they figure they have the best chance of obtaining a donation. If they want to run different approaches by you, just keep in mind the separation of the donor/vendor and the decision maker. Explain to leaders and managers—whoever challenges you on this—the problem of conflicts of interest and the appearance of conflicts of interest. Just like the physicians and the pizzas, the point is that sponsorship can be an influence on judgment, and there can be an appearance of such an influence.

Another area where vendors provide sponsorship support is through education. This can occur in various ways. A vendor may offer to pay for employees of your organization to attend a certain educational event or conference, usually one that the vendor is sponsoring. Your people will likely tell you that this event is valuable and that there is very good information there. (Sometimes they think it's not an important event, but they want to check anyhow.) So, the issue here is twofold: First, the vendor should not be choosing who goes to a conference; that is the organization's job. If the vendor is trying to woo the decision makers by wining and dining them at an event, that is the exact behavior we must avoid. The solution is for the vendor to make a donation to the company for education so that the company can decide who to send to events.

The second part is deciding whether the event is really educational. Check out the agenda to make sure it's not just a "boondoggle" sales event wrapped in overpriced dinners, drinks, and golf games. Are the presentations all about this vendor's products? Or have legitimate, independent speakers been lined up to present on topics of interest? Many leaders understand why this matters and often won't want to waste valuable time if otherwise. Others, depending on the organization, may not have actually considered the educational aspects but will understand the issue once you explain.

A variation on the sponsorship for education theme is when vendors pay physicians or other influential persons in the organization to speak at their events. You may never even hear about when a physician is so engaged, depending on that physician's relationship with the organization and the degree of understanding that medical staff leadership has about these issues.

If someone is invited to speak at an event, the first question to ask is what the topic is. Will the speaker be able to choose the presentation topic? If the vendor already has a topic picked and presentation lined up, the invitation to speak is much more likely to be problematic, because the vendor is probably having the physician or employee do a spiel that promotes the vendor's products or services. If that is the proposal, the answer is no.

Another question to ask is about the forum of the event. Will it be held at an overpriced resort, with more golf and drinking than actual presentations? If the physician or employee is invited for three days at a Florida resort where only three hours total of "education" is provided, you know this is not a legitimate conference.

Sometimes the event is legitimate, even if luxurious; and you believe that, for any number of reasons, it is beneficial for the person to accept the offer to speak. If that is the case, the employee should not get paid to attend while also getting speaker fees from the vendor.

If the event occurs over a weekend or otherwise on the employee's own time, that's different; but the employee should not be going on the company's dime and getting paid by each party. You can advise the vendor that any money for speaker fees goes to the company's foundation or fundraising department, or the employee can decline payment. Ultimately, your company needs to determine whether the engagement is truly a benefit to the organization and whether it's worth having this individual absent for that amount of time.

### *Discounts*

Discounts are challenging from a compliance perspective, because some arrangements that include free or discounted items may be acceptable, whereas others are considered kickbacks. Departments in your organization that negotiate purchasing arrangements should be advised that any arrangements that include free or discounted products or services need to be reviewed by the compliance officer or legal counsel, who is well versed in these matters. If you come into this role without experience reviewing such issues, it is an area to learn; or make sure you have a knowledgeable attorney to work with.

In general, the OIG believes that free items included "with purchase" are likely to be an inducement to purchase a vendor's products. However, in some situations this may be acceptable; for instance, if your organization buys a product and the vendor provides a device to administer that product for free. In other words, if the freebie can be used *solely* in conjunction with the item you are purchasing, it is acceptable, because it isn't providing a separate benefit to the purchaser.

Here's another example: You are working with a vendor to purchase a new electronic records system, and the vendor offers the system with a free iPad; that benefit is independent of the system you are buying. Yes, you can use the iPad to access electronic records offsite, so it can be used in conjunction with the product; but you can also use that iPad to watch movies, surf eBay, and do whatever else you might want to do with it, so it has value independent of the product being purchased. In this example, the freebie is not acceptable.

Discounts are tricky because the analysis of the arrangement is fact-specific. I recommend that you locate a good resource to have handy as you review arrangements. A number of good publications are available, and this is a complex area where the investment is worthwhile. It's also a topic that will likely result in pushback, because in some instances the free or discounted item provides a significant benefit to the organization and will be wanted.

In a time when margins are thin, this is not at all unreasonable; everyone needs to be aware of costs and getting as much valuable as possible out of purchases.

That is why it is critical to be very sure you know what you are doing and have good resources to help with discounts analysis. You don't want to cost the organization unnecessarily by being overcautious, but you also don't want it entering into inappropriate arrangements. If you are perceived as an impediment, it will discourage people from bringing such situations to your attention.

It also helps to be aware that vendors' competitors can and do blow the whistle and report these types of arrangements to the government; they have the most motivation to do so. You might point that out internally as part of your education about discounts and freebies. Proactively address the actual risks.

Remember, the tendency is to look at these types of issues from a cost/benefit perspective, and people who are primarily interested in watching the bottom line may believe that the risk is minimal and that the benefit outweighs any probability of harm. All you can do is make sure they are fully informed, and keep your own record of that guidance. In fact, keep records of all the guidance you provide; at some point you will be glad you did.

### Access

Vendors present another issue: their access to the facility, staff, physicians, and patients. First, the facility needs to control which vendors are on-site, who they meet with, and when. If you are in a large practice or hospital, this can be challenging unless you have a rigorous process and controls in place. Ironically, you can hire vendors to manage vendors. You can set up a system to subject vendors to a credentialing process and issue them access badges. Part of vendors' agreements with the facility is that they only arrive when they have an appointment, and they identify who they are there to see before being given access. In a small facility or practice, such a system is overkill, but I still recommend that you do some sort of background check or verification on who you let in. Sometimes, the company sending the vendor provides documentation or other assurance that this individual has been screened.

Access is an obvious security issue; you don't want vendors wandering the halls showing up at various practitioners' doors unannounced.

Vendor access is also an issue of patient privacy. Vendors typically don't have a legitimate reason to be in patient care areas or to have access to patient records. In very specific situations, a device manufacturer's vendor may be allowed in the surgical suite to observe or to guide the use of a specific device, but this should not be the norm. Also, vendors should not be allowed to "shadow" physicians or other practitioners. Vendors sometimes offer to pay physicians for this "preceptorship," when in fact it is buying time with the practitioner. This is not acceptable from the government's perspective; it is considered a potential kickback. And it is not acceptable from a compliance perspective because of the privacy issues and the kickback concerns.

Vendors should not attend meetings where patient cases are discussed unless there is a very good reason for them to be there; for instance, the device manufacturer is present to discuss specific cases involving its device. I've heard of cases where vendors brought doughnuts and routinely attended quality meetings where patient cases were discussed. They had been doing it for so long that it had become normal, and nobody thought anything about it until the privacy issue was raised. Obviously, the practice was discontinued immediately, but that is a good example of activities that can occur so routinely they aren't even questioned anymore.

To gain access to your facility, the vendor should agree to the following:

- It will follow organizational policies and procedures, as applicable, including any health and safety requirements.
- It will not attempt to access or solicit patients or patient information unless necessary to do its job, and with approval of the facility.
- It will not come to the facility without an appointment and will only meet with the scheduled person.

Have policies and procedures in place that address all of the above issues, and make sure that the Code of Conduct is consistent with those policies. As I said in the beginning, some of these issues will be debated very early on, when you draft the Code. The details, however, will be in the supporting policies, and the challenges could arise again.

As you work through the policies, make sure that you include key stakeholders from the Medical Executive Committee, Purchasing, and the Security department. In a smaller organization, make sure you discuss all these issues with the facility or practice leadership and key physicians so that everyone understands the issues and necessary processes.

Access is a huge training issue for everyone, from the front desk to the physicians. I have found it useful to attend department meetings to work through some of the logistics with Purchasing and, to the extent any issue involves fundraising, with the Development staff. Certainly, anyone with any sort of marketing role also needs to thoroughly understand vendor issues.

# CONTRACTS

When you think about many of the big fraud and abuse cases that make headlines, it should not be surprising that managing contracts and financial arrangements is on my list of special issues. Some of these issues were covered in the vendor discussion, but vendors are not the only risk.

Many compliance risks arise either in the terms of contracts or in the failure to properly manage or follow the documents. One very common example: Expired contracts with physicians can be a Stark violation, even though the oversight might be unintentional. It still surprises me how many organizations stuff their contracts into a desk drawer once they are negotiated and then virtually forget about them. That's scary for a variety of compliance and business reasons.

Your organization should have a centralized system for managing contracts. If it does not, you need to put this issue high up on your list of compliance projects.

Identify who in your organization is authorized to sign contracts, and then obtain copies of the agreements. A review of the contracts is appropriate and necessary at this point, particularly reviews of physician contracts and any other arrangements with potential referral sources.

There are many pieces to be aware of regarding contracts, so let's start with the actual management of the documents.

Contract management begins with a documented approval process. If you are in a small company, this is not a big problem: A contract review checklist is created, and the chief executive or whoever does the contracting ultimately signs off on the contract. Ideally, as the compliance officer you will have a role in the process, as well, to serve as a "check and balance" function. Even in a small practice, there should be some form of controls over the contracts entered into, so keep this in mind as you develop a contract management policy and procedure. Maybe the controls consist of a review by the leadership team, the compliance officer, and counsel, or some other structure; but more than just one person should enter into and sign off on contracts. In addition, the person seeking to bring in the product or service should not be the one who ultimately reviews and approves the agreement, because in that scenario there are no checks and balances.

In large organizations, start by asking for a contract authority matrix. Companies or health systems with multiple departments and locations should have a document that identifies who in the organization has the authority to enter into contracts on behalf of the company. This is an important control, and if the company is large enough to warrant such a document but does not have one, there should be help for you to get it in place. Frequently, the Finance department, with leadership approval, is in charge of developing the list of people with contract authority. Internal Audit should also consult on this process. The contracts approval process might also include levels of approval, depending on the dollar value or type of arrangement.

The next tool you need in place is a contract review and approval checklist. You might have more than one version in a large health system, because different types of agreements have different requirements. A lease arrangement, for instance, carries different risks than an agreement for purchasing capital equipment or bringing in a medical director. The checklist should include the key risk issues that need to be reviewed for the arrangement and should have more than one person sign off.

The next thing to consider is how you will track agreements. In small practices, this isn't terribly complicated; you can set up an Excel spreadsheet. In large organizations, you can purchase a product that manages your agreements, sends notifications, and does a variety of related functions. Some tools can also manage policies, so it's worth researching before buying any document management system to make sure it addresses as many of your needs as possible for the best price. Not only that, but we all have too many passwords to remember, so simpler is always best!

Regardless of how you decide to manage your agreements, certain pieces of information must be included:

- Vendor or company/physician name
- Type of agreement (lease, medical director, etc.)
- Contract owner (who signs it?)
- Effective date
- Expiration date
- Business associate (yes or no?)

If related documents need to be maintained, the system should also include reminders and expiration dates for those documents. Proof of insurance is an example for a contract in which the other party needs to carry and provide proof of insurance. For contracts with referral sources, documentation showing fair market determinations must be maintained. One advantage of buying a contract management system is that you can scan in all the accessory documents, which does make it easier to maintain the files and to sort and pull them without much effort.

In terms of tracking renewals, make sure the in-house process starts working on the review and renewal at least ninety days in advance, especially for physician arrangements and other contracts for which the terms may change and negotiation may take time. Although one advantage of "evergreen" clauses (that renew contracts automatically) is that contracts don't expire, these contracts lend themselves to a lack of routine review, which can cause other types of problems. My preference is to stay away from evergreen contracts and to perform routine contract reviews and renewals; this helps ensure that the services or supplies are still needed and that the terms are still acceptable.

I have witnessed situations when evergreen contracts were stuffed in a drawer somewhere, and the company was paying for the services; but nobody even knew about it, and the company was losing money every month. This is one huge reason for managing contracts, and it's one that you can raise with leadership if you get pushback on trying to corral the contracts: The organization can save money if you actively manage and review arrangements.

Attorneys manage the actual contracts, but compliance officers should be aware of certain factors. You should be familiar with business associate agreements. Many organizations don't understand who is and who is not a business associate, so they don't secure these agreements when they should. Under HIPAA, a business associate is any individual or organization that performs services on behalf of the covered entity that involve the use or disclosure of protected health information. Although not every person or organization is a business associate, it is never a bad idea to include language in agreements that states that the other party will comply with all laws, rules, and regulations pertaining to the privacy and security of patient health information and will sign a business associate agreement if appropriate. Legal counsel usually has boilerplate to put in contracts. This is something to watch for if you are involved in contract reviews.

Another item a compliance officer wants to see in agreements is the right for the company to review the other party's processes or records that relate to the services being provided. This is important to verify not only HIPAA compliance, but also compliance in general. Say, for instance, you think there might be a compliance problem with a billing company. You want the right to audit the company and its processes. This is mostly relevant to arrangements in which a vendor provides services on your behalf rather than purchasing agreements. The bottom line is this: If an outside organization could create a compliance issue for you, you should have the right to audit it, review its processes to verify compliance, or both.

# ATTORNEYS

As a compliance officer, you will spend quality time with the company attorneys, in-house counsel, outside counsel, or perhaps both. This is true even if you are an attorney yourself, because a compliance officer who is an attorney is not acting in the capacity of an attorney. It's important to keep this distinction in mind so as to prevent employees from mistakenly taking your compliance guidance as legal advice. Be sure to educate people in the organization about your role.

In small companies that don't have in-house counsel, someone in the organization will come to you for legal advice. I typically remind people that I can give advice only in my role as the compliance officer and that, if they need legal assistance, they should talk to the organization's attorney. This is particularly relevant for technical, high-risk issues like potential Stark violations or complex financial arrangements. I don't want to be responsible for offering legal advice that is outside my scope, and you don't, either.

Explain that you could get in trouble for providing legal advice when you have not been retained as counsel; people typically understand that, but they ask anyhow. Granted, the lines between Compliance and Legal are often blurred; for instance, when it comes to reviewing contracts, so you don't want to go too far with this and not do your job, but you do need to be very clear about your scope. If you are corresponding electronically, I recommend adding a disclaimer that explains messages do not constitute legal advice and that employees should discuss issues with counsel. (If you are an attorney in the Compliance role, none of this is news to you, but I want to be overinclusive.)

This is not the reason I have included a whole section on attorneys, however. Rather, I want to discuss the issues of attorney-client privilege and work-product privilege, which are rules of evidence. These issues, frequently misunderstood, can and do arise with some regularity in relation to internal reviews, audits, and investigations. Sometimes concern over privileges is appropriately raised before an audit; in other cases, it is mentioned after an audit is underway or even has been completed. It is important for you to understand the appropriate use of the privileges to best protect the organization. At some point, people will want to privilege some activity, and many times they don't understand how or when the privileges apply.

### *Attorney-Client Privilege*

The purpose of the attorney-client privilege is to protect communications between the attorney and the client; protected communications occur for purposes of securing legal advice. One important aspect of this privilege is that it is related to legal advice only. That may seem obvious, but many times the attorney, especially one acting as in-house counsel, is asked to weigh in on matters that cross over into business advice. Business guidance is not privileged.

It is also important to understand that the communications between the attorney and the client are privileged. Remember this point, because it will come up as soon as someone in the organization does an audit and finds something alarming. This person will immediately suggest that the attorney be brought in and the audit and the related files or claims be privileged. No, no, no. Facts are not privileged, only the *communications* with the attorney are subject to privilege, and only if the purpose is for securing legal advice.

If it seems that I am beating on this point, it is because I have seen inappropriate use of privilege attempted far too many times. So, in this example of a negative audit, you might send a memo or have a conversation with the attorney about the audit and how to handle the issue going forward. But the underlying facts themselves cannot be hidden by labeling them as privileged. Attorney-client privilege does not apply to facts, as I just explained.

In addition, in this example there is the issue of attempting to privilege communications or activities after the fact. When an employee comes to you with a situation similar to the one above (and they will), you need to advise them that you can't apply privilege retroactively. I can't tell you how many otherwise well-informed people in leadership roles have tried this and truly did not know that they couldn't just call something privileged after the fact.

The other issue that sometimes comes up with attorney-client privilege is the question of "who is the client?" In short, the organization is the client, and the attorney is working on behalf of the organization. This is important to distinguish, because at times employees have the idea that the company attorney is supposed to protect them. If there is an investigation and legal counsel is leading it, they should advise the employees of this fact to avoid confusion. A nervous employee may come to you, however, and ask the question, so it's good for you to know the answer: The attorney's duty of loyalty is to the corporation. If employees have questions about their own legal protection, they should discuss the matter with the company attorney, who can best explain it to them.

### *Attorney Work-Product Privilege*

Many times you will see a document labeled as both attorney-client privileged and attorney work-product privileged. So, what is the difference? Attorney work-product privilege applies to documents and files that were prepared in anticipation of litigation in order to protect those documents from review by opposing counsel. One important point here is that the files need not be created by the attorney, but rather may be work product generated by individuals working on behalf of the attorney, under his or her direction.

This privilege is where confusion most often arises with respect to "who is the client?" because you may have an investigation in which the Compliance department or Internal Audit does a review and interviews employees as part of the process. There is no attorney in the room; the attorney has given direction on the activity and is, in effect, supervising it. The employees then may be confused about the privilege and who it applies to. The employees, auditors, or consultants who are doing the audit need to advise employees at the beginning of each interview that the activity is privileged and confidential and is being directed by counsel. The interviewee needs to understand that the person doing the interview is acting on behalf of the attorney, and that the organization is the client. It is confusing to average employees, because they expect to see the lawyer in the room when something is "privileged."

That leads to another source of bewilderment: "Who is the attorney when Compliance or Internal Audit is conducting the review?" People need to understand that the person doing the review on behalf of the attorney is the same as the attorney with respect to privilege. So, that auditor's documentation is protected by attorney work-product privilege because the review is being directed by counsel.

Perhaps these issues seem obvious to you; but you need to really understand how this works, because in complex audits with many moving parts, people will be nervous and will seek understanding and assurances of who is doing what, and why, and how they are protected. It's a normal response, but one you should be prepared to deal with. The Compliance department is not the client. The employee is not the client. The corporation is the client.

### *Applying the Privileges*

In many situations, the two types of privileges work together. For instance, a complaint might be lodged that documentation is being falsified to enhance coding and billing. The individual might also allege that he or she reported the concern previously and was then retaliated against. The person might also claim to have spoken to an attorney already.

You (appropriately) go to legal counsel to discuss the issue and get legal advice on how best to proceed.

The attorney recommends that you do a review and that he or she directs it in order to put the review under attorney-client and attorney work-product privilege. Counsel might also suggest that outside counsel be retained to lead the review, depending on the issue and how the in-house Legal department typically operates.

The review is conducted in anticipation of litigation, because the employee has spoken with an attorney and because the potential for False Claims Act violations means the government may be involved later. In addition, the review is protected by attorney-client privilege because the audit and related work is being conducted to secure the attorney's guidance on how to manage the issue legally. In this instance, it is appropriate to label all documents created during this process as "subject to attorney-client and attorney work-product privilege" or whatever similar language your legal counsel prefers to use.

This example is a clear-cut case where legal counsel should be involved, and its role is clear; but many situations are not as obvious. So, when should the privileges *not* apply?

One time is in situations where the purpose of an activity is not related to seeking legal guidance. As I suggested earlier, this may seem more obvious in the abstract than it does in reality. In-house attorneys often are a valuable source of business guidance, and the lines can become blurry. If you are involved in an issue where someone suggests it be privileged, ask this question first: Is this related to seeking legal advice?

Routine audits and reviews are frequently misunderstood in relation to the appropriate use of privilege. Many individuals believe that any activity involving audits should be privileged, even if the audits are part of the ordinary course of business. This is the second-most frequent debate I have been involved in related to the application of attorney-client/work-product privilege. If an activity is routine, for instance, an annual audit that is part of your work plan, it is not being conducted in anticipation of litigation, and it is not being done for purposes of obtaining legal advice. It just isn't.

Stand your ground on this one because misuse of privilege weakens it generally; and if the government challenges the privilege, you will lose credibility and appear to be uncooperative and hiding information. That is not the message you want to send to the government. Save the use of privilege for cases where it is truly necessary and appropriate.

One question that is not asked often enough is whether an activity should even be privileged. As I have stated, trying to overuse privilege can cause a lot more harm than it prevents. When one of these situations comes up, have a conversation with the attorney and the business leader or executive who is involved or who is pushing for privilege. The first point of discussion is to ask why it should be privileged.

For instance, if you think there may be an overpayment, the knee-jerk response is to privilege the audit. Why would you want to do that? Unless there is a reasonable belief that the issue is more than an unintentional mistake (i.e., fraud), the organization will simply be repaying any identified overpayment. This is required by law, so repayment is not really an issue for which legal advice needs to be sought. (It's always good to touch base with counsel, I'm not saying otherwise. Just that routine issues don't necessarily justify asserting privilege.) The organization discloses to the government payers that it's identified the issue and will pay back the money, along with the details of how the overpayment was found and quantified and how future occurrences are being prevented. Because you must do that by law, what exactly do you need to protect with privilege? The same logic holds true for most issues that are routine or errors.

If the executives understand the legal requirements regarding overpayments and still push for privilege because they don't intend to pay them back, well, you have a bigger problem, which we discuss in the section on corporate culture.

What happens when that routine audit reveals a concerning problem? This is *the* most common debate I have had regarding privilege, which is the ability to protect an audit after the fact by bringing in the attorney and calling it privileged. For all the reasons I discussed earlier, it doesn't work like that. It is, however, sometimes appropriate at this point to have a discussion with the attorney about how to manage the identified issue going forward. This is seeking legal guidance, so it's appropriate. If the attorney determines that additional reviews or an investigation is justified, then that work can be subject to the attorney work-product privilege and attorney-client privilege, provided that you properly retain the attorney. Certainly, if there is any indication of fraud and abuse or other serious wrongdoing, then the attorney should be immediately involved.

To put a review or investigation under privilege, the fact that the attorney is leading the activity and has been "engaged" or "retained" for that purpose must be documented. The importance of this cannot be overstated: Having an attorney in the same building, organization, or even office does not create an automatic privilege. In addition, having a compliance officer with a law degree does not confer privilege on reviews.

You might be surprised at the misconceptions surrounding this matter. I have heard seasoned executives state during phone calls that because one of the individuals on the call is an attorney, the conversation is privileged. First, the lawyer on the call was not working as an attorney for the company but was in a different role. Second, just being on a call does not create privilege. It would be laughable if it wasn't such a common belief.

To establish the attorney's role in an issue, you should have an engagement letter or documentation. Your legal department or outside counsel will most likely have a template, but if not, you can draft such a document; it's not complicated. You need to include the following information:

- Who is retaining the attorney (organization name)
- For what purpose (for example, "providing legal direction relating to an audit of the Wound Center and the management of identified issues")
- Effective date
- The attorney's role (for example, "The purpose of this letter is to engage Attorney X to lead a review and resolution of XYZ issue")

The main takeaways here are twofold: Get documentation that the attorney has been engaged for the specific matter, *and* make sure this engagement is drafted and finalized *prior* to beginning any audit or investigation you intend to protect with privilege.

If you are using in-house counsel, you can use an email, although be sure that it comes from someone with the right level of authority. If you have authority to retain counsel, then you can do it, or the chief executive can do it. Just don't let the CEO have a secretary or a low-level auditor send it. Remember, the corporation is the client, so whoever engages the attorney needs to be able to speak for the company and make decisions on behalf of the organization.

Once you have sufficiently established privilege, you need to make sure it's maintained. This is an issue that requires ongoing monitoring, because when a review or investigation is being conducted, everyone will want to discuss it and know what's going on.

The first step to maintaining privilege is establishing who specifically the "client" is for purposes of communication. This needs to be a very small group, and only those in that group receive communication regarding the status of the activity. It would be appropriate, for instance, to have the CEO, the compliance officer, and the business leader involved in the issue to be included. It is *not* appropriate to copy everyone who may have an interest in the issue, and this is a danger that all involved parties need to be educated about. Email has become such a normal way of communicating, and it is so easy to forward or reply to all and have an email sent out all over the organization.

This is a very common occurrence, not surprisingly. Say, for instance, there is a problem in the Wound Center. The director of the Wound Center is involved in the investigation (assuming, of course, this person is not suspected as part of the problem). An attorney-led audit is performed, and several compliance issues are detected. When the Wound Center director finds out, he or she immediately wants to fix the problems. It would be natural for that director to forward the audit report to the management team, with a request for a meeting to discuss how to resolve the issues. This person is trying to do a proper job of correcting a compliance issue.

To take this a step further, perhaps the Wound Center outsources the coding or billing function. Perhaps it has residents in the department part of the time. You can see how this can quickly take on a life of its own, and pretty soon the organization has effectively waived the privilege. Not to mention the fact that, if you do have a bad actor in the department, this person is now in the know about what is going on and may cause further damage.

There should be an initial meeting prior to the start of the investigation, and if the attorney doesn't bring up this issue, you should. Ask the attorney who needs to be included in any communications. You can include this list in the engagement documentation if you choose.

The next step in maintaining privilege is to know that when you are acting under the attorney's direction, your reports go to the attorney first, not to the client. It is normal for the business unit leader to ask you what you are finding before the process has gone through proper channels. Before you talk with anyone, discuss with the attorney how much you should tell other stakeholders throughout the process. It is completely understandable that they want to know; it is their department. They should understand, however, that it isn't up to you what you share and when, because you are acting on behalf of counsel. Provide people with assurances that you will check in with the attorney and get back to them right away, one way or the other. If you put yourself in their shoes, you will understand how nerve-wracking it is for them and why they want to know right away.

You have to consider how people not on the "client" team handle any information they receive. Say, for instance, an employee has been violating department policy. If the report isn't finalized and the attorney has not provided guidance, you don't want the leader of that function going to Human Resources and taking action. Management should not do anything until counsel agrees. Restraining leaders in this situation can be next to impossible, which is one reason it's best to make sure communications come directly from the attorney so that a good discussion of next steps can happen before the leader goes off to try to "fix" the issue.

Maintain privilege also by instructing individuals involved in the investigation, that is, the "witnesses," to keep relevant information confidential. People may be scared or may just want to talk about the problem to gossip or be in the know. They may think that they can ask around and get more information, or maybe they just want to tell that *one* person they *know* will keep it to themselves. I wish there was a magic bullet for preventing this, but the best you can do is to be very clear and direct about the confidentiality of the process and the risk to employees and the organization if they disclose information inappropriately.

Be sure to mark documents and communications appropriately as privileged and confidential. Don't comingle privileged documentation with other types of records. Be sure to keep privileged documentation together, and secured.

# CORPORATE CULTURE

Corporate culture may seem like a soft topic, but it can truly make or break the efforts of a compliance officer. My main purpose is to make you aware of cultural issues and show you how they can affect your success. An organization's culture exemplifies the manner in which the company expects its employees to conduct themselves. It can be explicitly stated, as a point of differentiating the company from other organizations, or it can be more subtle, learned as you go.

Consider a conservative CPA or law firm; you can tell as soon as you walk in the door what the expectation is, as you see how people are dressed and how they conduct themselves. If you were to join that organization, you probably wouldn't walk in on your first day in a flaming-pink suit and silver stilettos; it's just not a good plan if you want to fit in. In all probability nobody has to really explain the culture to you, either.

Although culture can be a selling point during an interview—think: "We value integrity, respect, and transparency, in all our employees"—it can turn out that the actual culture is not what is represented; your experience of the corporate culture might not quite match up to the hiring spiel.

If you are moving into a compliance role but have already worked in the organization, you have a good understanding of the organizational culture already. If you are new to the company, then this is just one more item to add to your list to incorporate into your new role.

The Compliance department is often viewed as a cost center that doesn't produce revenue. It is also perceived to be the reason why many moves that make business sense are not happening (think about some of the issues discussed in the section on vendors). No matter how supportive leadership is, some individuals will hold these beliefs, and it will be tough to change their convictions. The problem is, however, if this opinion is widely held at the leadership level, you will find challenges arising on a regular basis. The oft-quoted mantra about the "tone at the top" is more than just rhetoric; it makes a huge difference, especially for compliance officers.

So, what are some warning signs that you are getting involved in an organization that doesn't support

Compliance? One prominent red flag is organizations that have had turnover in the Compliance department. One compliance officer whose tenure was short isn't necessarily an indication of high turnover, but if there is a pattern of it, you should try to find out why.

If the department has staff who have been around through the changes, they can give you their input about what caused those turnovers. Administrative support people usually know a lot about what goes on, even if they are discreet and don't say anything. People watch and listen, and if you think the turnover has been unusual, you might want to find out why. If one person causes problems, you might not be able to do anything to prevent it. Or you can try to develop a relationship with that person and perhaps learn what the issues are. Maybe you can even change this person's behavior if you find a way to "convert" him or her! As you cultivate relationships, watch and listen. Someone will likely feel the need to inform you of what's been going on, or at least what they perceive has happened. It can be valuable information to have. Just be sure to keep in mind the possible motivations of your 'informant', and evaluate all information accordingly.

If the culture problem is at the board and executive level, however, you do have a test ahead. Although most leaders say they support Compliance, pay attention to the subtext to ascertain how they really feel. They might make comments about the cost of compliance, the lack of benefits, and other remarks that clearly show leadership's disdain for your function.

One way that this creates problems for you is that leaders may not support or approve various initiatives. For instance, perhaps you join an organization that in the past has only done conflict of interest disclosures for board members. You see this as an area where you should change the policy and procedure to include all management, leaders, physicians, and anyone who has contracting or prescribing authority. The leadership team refuses because they see this as excessive and irritating to the physicians. Or maybe they allow you to move forward but put a number of barriers in your way, such as a multilayer approval process for every stage of the development. At this point, you start to glean the reason for the turnover in the compliance role.

Another cultural challenge arises when people complain, as they inevitably do, to the CEO or other leader about compliance-related activities or policies. In a culture that is supportive of Compliance, the leader stops complaints right away and reinforces the fact that the organization is committed to an effective compliance program. Even if leaders hear something that doesn't sound quite right, they should not undermine Compliance, although they should assure the complainer that they will find out what is going on. In a difficult corporate culture, the leader might say something about having to do this Compliance thing and that they understand it's a pain, or words to that effect. That is when the tone at the top really becomes your enemy, and you start noticing resistance, even if it's passive resistance—people don't respond to your surveys, conflict of interest disclosure requests, policy reviews, and other requests, and they stall, putting roadblocks in your way. They know leadership doesn't like Compliance, either, so they know that your activities are not a priority that they need to worry about.

When you encounter pushback over a Compliance initiative, you should be able to state with confidence that the Compliance Committee and the board approved and agrees with the activity. If you can't say that with certainty, it isn't realistic to expect the employees to fall in line if they don't want to.

In a supportive culture, you can report on Compliance activities to the board or board committee without being censored. Censorship is another strategy for keeping Compliance in line: having management or leadership review your board reports and "approve" or require changes before you can present them. When this happens, it usually means that management won't allow full transparency with the board. In a supportive culture, management and leadership should *see* your report in advance and *should* mentor you about the content. You don't want to take a report to the board that is unintentionally inflammatory so that it distracts from the content.

If you haven't done board reporting before, it's especially reasonable to get plenty of review and feedback from leadership. But don't let them tell you, for instance, to skip including a compliance audit with a high error rate or notice of an OIG investigation. These directions warrant asking the question "Why?" or "Why not?"

Remember, your job is to be objective. That stance isn't always popular, and sometimes it makes certain people look bad. If leadership doesn't value the necessity of objectivity in your role, the culture may be tainted against Compliance.

As the compliance officer, it is your job to thoroughly educate the board and leadership about the role of Compliance, the benefits to the organization, and the role the compliance officer plays in supporting the company and its mission. If you can deliver this message effectively, you can help create a tone at the top that understands the full scope of compliance and the potential impact if it isn't supported. If you have provided comprehensive education and still aren't getting support from leadership, you have a definite cultural problem.

So, what do you do? I'm afraid there isn't a surefire answer, no miracle drug. Mainly, do not compromise your integrity. This can be a formidable task if you, like most people, need your paycheck! I recommend giving your all to get leadership to change its attitude, but you have to approach this carefully or you will do irreparable damage to the relationship. It is possible that you may not be able to improve the situation; others before you may have also tried and failed. But so long as you don't disregard your principles, you will have the comfort of virtue and knowing that your professional reputation will not be compromised. The organization may have had a bad experience with a compliance officer who didn't work in a collaborative fashion; if that is the cause, you may be able to turn it around with time and patience.

As a new compliance officer, you might not be sure what the boundaries are between being coached and being censored. All I can say is that, if something doesn't feel right, find an experienced compliance person in your network and ask for advice. It's always best to get an objective opinion when you're not sure. Sometimes a third party can easily tell you that there is no issue and really you're just working with a micromanager who won't ultimately interfere with your job performance or autonomy. Sometimes people just doesn't understand how your role works and are nervous.

When you start a new job, it's not usually easy to detect culture problems on the front end. It's not like you can assess the issue with a survey; leaders will always tell you that the organization is all about doing the right thing. You just need to pay attention and listen to what is being said in comparison to what is carried out.

Another point to know: An organization that has experienced real compliance problems most likely has found religion. In organizations that have been subject to costly government settlements, huge privacy breaches, or Corporate Integrity Agreements, most leadership teams are on board with Compliance! They may not like it, but they have come to understand it.

One last point about culture: Be aware of culture problems becoming a true compliance issue. Sometimes you will receive complaints about a hostile work environment or retaliation and you don't find any actual violation when you investigate (or when HR investigates). If there are a lot of those sorts of complaints, however, it can indicate a culture problem, even if only in a particular department. If left unchecked, these sorts of issues can continue escalating until they become a true compliance issue and create organizational risk. Be aware of those complaints that don't trigger a compliance finding; trends should never be ignored. It's a good idea to look at policies and training that management and leaders have received around retaliation, etc., if you start seeing this type of pattern.

# MERGERS, CONSOLIDATIONS, AND ACQUISITIONS

A MERGER OCCURS WHEN TWO companies join together and one "survives," that is, it absorbs the other. A consolidation, on the other hand, is when organizations combine and together create a totally new company. Acquisitions occur when one organization "buys" and assumes control over another. In all cases, each organization needs to review aspects of the other's business to ensure that it is not taking on an association that will create unexpected risks, liabilities, or other unwanted problems; this is commonly referred to as due diligence. Due diligence is appropriate for a variety of other arrangements, too, including affiliation and joint venture arrangements. In any of these scenarios, your organization wants to know about the other business before spending money or assuming new risks.

Compliance plays a role in organizational mergers, acquisitions, and other business arrangements in the context of due diligence. Whether you are part of a health system merger, a physician practice that is partnering with or being bought by a hospital, or some other partnership or collaboration, there are multiple potential compliance risks and considerations. The presence of liabilities can affect how the transaction is structured, who will assume liability, or even if both organizations are willing to go forward. Many types of potential liabilities must be considered, including:

- Referral arrangements (Stark and Anti-Kickback concerns)
- HIPAA privacy and security, and related state laws
- Documentation, billing, and coding
- Past or current government audits or investigations, including those for fraud and abuse, documentation and coding, medical necessity, and quality of care
- Accreditation and licensure
- Meaningful use
- Discounts, bad debt, and charity care processes

Compliance should be involved in due diligence from the inception of these types of transactions. Due diligence typically involves a thorough review of financial statements, performance history, and other business-related issues to ensure that both parties are comfortable with moving forward. If a hospital is buying a physician practice, it wants a valuation of that practice. Such components are expected, but including Compliance is not always an assumed part of due diligence.

As the compliance officer, if an organization is potentially a party to these types of transactions, one of the discussions you should have with leadership in the very beginning of your time there is about due diligence and your role in it.

Several aspects of a Compliance review during due diligence identify the types of risks identified above:

- An assessment of the compliance program itself: Does one exist? Is it effective in practice? Does it actively assess and address risks, and if so, how? What are the results of the past risk assessments?
- Have there been any government audits and investigations? What was the outcome? What were the issues, and how have they been resolved? Were there overpayments?
- Does the organization have good documentation, coding, and billing practices? Can

any recent audits be reviewed? How are the coding and billing functions staffed and structured? Are the staff credentialed?

- What are the financial arrangements that are in place, especially with physicians and referral sources? How are those monitored from a Compliance perspective?
- Is there a privacy and security program in place? Have there been any breaches, and if so, how were they handled?
- Are there identified individuals accountable for compliance, privacy, and security? What are their backgrounds or credentials?

These are some of the core issues to explore. This may include reviewing the documentation and coding or perhaps the financial arrangements. If the organization was subject to audits or reviews by the government or other payers, you may want to review the issues raised during those processes to confirm that it truly has been resolved. The Financial and Legal teams will be looking at the financial and business risks, but the valuation—or even the deal itself—can be affected by significant compliance issues that create liability.

The compliance officer's work is not done when due diligence is complete. In some cases, in fact, due diligence may be the simplest part of the transaction and transition.

In mergers and acquisitions, the compliance officer must next question how the compliance and privacy/security programs of the entities will be combined. It can be straightforward or messy, depending on the size and nature of the parties and on the strength of the compliance programs. If, for instance, a large hospital is buying a small physician practice, it is expected that the hospital's compliance and privacy/security program will absorb the practice's and will take responsibility for compliance. If a designated person manages compliance, you can educate that person about the larger organization's policies, procedures, and programs. The physician practice may have good processes in place, such as a routine monitoring and auditing process, and these might best be incorporated into the new combined compliance program.

In the event two large organizations come together, it can be much more complicated. Not only do you have to find a way to combine two programs, you also have to deal with the question of who will lead the effort. This may have been negotiated on the front end, but it is equally likely that the decision about structuring Compliance was not negotiated.

If that is the case, the due diligence process may have identified a weak compliance program, and presumably the decision for the better-developed program to lead should be straightforward. But what if both programs seem to be roughly equivalent? Each compliance officer may believe his or her program should be adopted because it is stronger or the organization is larger. This happens quite often, so don't be surprised.

A potential solution is to have an external assessment done of both programs to identify best practices. Although this might not be an expense either organization wants to incur, an outside evaluation can uncover strengths and weaknesses so that the Compliance departments can collaborate to create the best possible program using the finest parts from each organization.

Given the potential friction on this issue, an independent opinion may be well worth the money spent, particularly because it will result in recommendations for a "best practice" program. It is natural for the architect of each program to believe his or hers is superior, so having an objective third party evaluate the various components can be the best option.

An advantage of such a review is that it also provides leverage to adopt best practices that may be sticking points with some leadership members. The more conservative organization may debate from that perspective. And if the new leadership agrees to adopt the review's recommendations, Compliance may end up in a stronger position for going forward successfully.

The actual integration of Compliance departments must be considered. The joined organizations need to determine not only who will be the compliance officer for the combined entity, but also who will staff the department and how it will be structured. Do what you can to ensure that the decision is made in a fair and equitable way and that both organizations are given a "seat at the table" for discussions about how to move forward.

Although you probably are not in the position to make this decision, depending on how it plays out, you may need to think about the aftereffects if it isn't handled correctly. There can be hurt feelings and resentment, there can be loss of valuable employees, passive resistance, and a variety of other challenges when the staff of one organization believe they have not been treated fairly. This obviously is not just a compliance program issue, but I think it may happen more often in Compliance because it is not an area that is often given much attention at the time of a merger in terms of future program structure.

Regardless, it's important to be aware that this can happen; and, if you have employees under you, try to advocate for them and for your department on the front end if it seems like Compliance is not being considered. During the initial integration process, what often happens is that a lot of focus is trained on Human Resources (for obvious reasons), Finance, the board and board committees, and clinical leadership, and the other departments are put in the back seat as the critical functions get sorted out. It's not possible to do everything at once, of course; but if you find this is occurring and make efforts to work out a collaborative relationship with the other compliance program employees, it will help tremendously. Just don't assume your program is superior, or that you should be the leader, even if it seems obvious to you. A lack of sensitivity can end up costing very good employees.

Last, if you are elected to be the new compliance officer of this revamped organization, make sure that you have a current and accurate organization chart that includes all the entities and lines of business. When two complex organizations join, you may become responsible for subordinate organizations or joint ventures, and so forth, that you aren't aware of. Make sure you know the scope of your new responsibilities whenever transactions can affect your role.

# HEALTH SYSTEMS

Although there are many types of healthcare organizations with unique requirements, I want to discuss health systems in particular because they present issues that can be tricky or can catch you unawares.

The first issue relates to joint ventures and other business arrangements, such as those referenced in the last section. The concern I am raising here, however, has to do with your responsibility for compliance and privacy in those organizations.

If you are hired to oversee Compliance for a health system, the first thing to know is the scope of that responsibility. What are all of the lines of business, functions, subsidiaries, and so forth that come under the corporate umbrella? You may think you know, only to find out otherwise at the most inopportune moment. When you start in a Compliance oversight role in a health system, be sure to get the organization chart, and specifically ask about other business interests that may come under your purview. It is quite likely that nobody has even thought about compliance for that entity—but they will as soon as there is a problem.

A variation on this theme is when your organization has a management service agreement in which the corporation has agreed to provide management services for another entity, whether owned or not. Ask about these types of arrangements, and if there are any, ask to read the agreements. You need to verify whether the management of Compliance is included and nobody has paid any attention to that detail. It's not at all uncommon.

If you find that you have additional compliance responsibilities, that raises the obvious question of how to fulfill these obligations. Depending on the amount of resources at your disposal, the size of your budget, and the amount of additional work, this may be a conversation you need to have with your leadership. What you absolutely do not want is to be responsible for compliance in these other entities without knowing it or without the resources to fill that role.

Another issue that comes up in large organizations such as health systems is program structure. One individual should be given overall responsibility for Compliance, but large organizations require more than one. Because Compliance really should be part of operations, not a purely corporate-level function, the various entities should have resources.

In a health system, that means there should be a compliance officer or director at the entity level and that this person reports either directly or indirectly to the corporate compliance officer. This is a full-time role. If you have any voice in the structure, try to have the entity-level person report to you (some organizations push back against this). If the entity compliance officer reports to the local organization, he or she can be pulled off for other priorities, or your work plan initiatives can be overridden. This is particularly true of part-time persons because then, in all likelihood, Compliance will take a back seat to other operational responsibilities.

When the Compliance staff across the system don't report to you, it means you will be challenged to meet your annual work plan goals because you need those individuals to do their share of the work. In this scenario, you are held accountable but don't have the authority to align your resources for the work. If this is your situation, discuss your concerns with the leader, and see what kind of resolution you can achieve. It may be that your work plan will only include the work your office does, and each entity will have their own work plans that roll up to the corporate office. Or the organization may change the reporting structure, although it isn't easy to achieve that outcome. In either case, just be aware of the potential challenges of this type of structure.

Another issue to be aware of in large health systems is that plenty of functional areas fall outside your area of expertise or experience. Maybe you don't know much about clinical laboratories, or research, or pharmacy; they all have very specific regulatory requirements. The best way to make sure risks are properly reviewed and managed is by having a Compliance liaison for functional areas with unique requirements, as mentioned earlier. This individual may not be a dedicated full-time Compliance resource, but the role should be added to the person's job description, and the liaison will be considered part of the Compliance team. You will find it easier to move ahead on initiatives involving areas with specialized requirements if a subject-matter expert in that function is involved.

If you are successful at establishing Compliance resources at the entity level and within key functional areas, you will find your work is much easier. Your job will not require as many resources directly under you if Compliance is distributed across the organization. The key is to document compliance responsibilities of compliance resources (such as in job descriptions), keep your resources involved, and make sure that all Compliance activities are reported up to the board or board committee to ensure accountability. Optimally, you can bring all of these individuals together on a regular basis to keep communication open and to facilitate information sharing and collaboration across entities and functions. This is more of a workgroup structure, not the operational Compliance Committee, and it really enhances your ability to be successful in a large health system.

# BOARD REPORTING

Although board reporting is at the end of the book, it is certainly not last in terms of importance. Board reporting is one of the most critical roles a compliance officer fills, and it can be the most intimidating for someone who has not performed this function in the past. As I mentioned earlier, compliance officers should have a reporting relationship with the board or board committee.

Use of the term *Compliance Committee* may cause some confusion. Boards, particularly in large organizations, have various committees that report up to them. This way, they can staff the committees with individuals best suited to assess and advise on those functions. Examples of committees include Quality, Finance, Audit, and Compliance. The Compliance Committee of the board is separate and distinct from the Compliance Committee that you chair that comprises operational leaders.

When discussing your program structure, be careful to distinguish the *board* Compliance Committee from the *operational* Compliance Committee. I have seen this confusion lead to a variety of misunderstandings. When you are aware of this issue, you can be sure to clarify in discussions. You might also need to educate people in your organization, perhaps even the chief executive, if he or she has not been involved in a compliance program before.

So, why is the board so important for Compliance? The first and probably most obvious reason is that the board sets the ultimate tone at the top. Your authority as a compliance officer derives from the board, and you need to be engaged with that body to ensure that you have support at the highest level. Board members have a duty of care that includes decision making and oversight. The government, and the Health and Human Services OIG in particular, has published a number of documents outlining these expectations:

- *Practical Guidance for Health Care Governing Boards on Compliance Oversight* (April 2015)
- *A Toolkit for Health Care Boards* (February 2012)
- *Corporate Responsibility and Health Care Quality: A Resource for Health Care Boards of Directors* (September 2007)

- *An Integrated Approach to Corporate Compliance: A Resource for Health Care Boards of Directors* (July 2004)
- *Corporate Responsibility and Corporate Compliance: A Resource for Health Care Boards of Directors* (April 2003)

Familiarize yourself with these documents, optimally before your first foray into the boardroom, and incorporate some of the key pieces into your first presentation. They can all be found on the HHS OIG website, along with many other useful resources.

Board members can be held personally liable for failing in their duties. One important case to look into is the *Caremark*[2] case, in which a shareholder sued the board of directors for a breach of the fiduciary duty of care. There is a trend toward holding organizational leaders, and even employees, personally responsible for serious violations of state and federal laws.

One development that you should be aware of is a publication by the U.S. Deputy Attorney General Sally Yates, which was released in 2015, known as the Yates Memo or the Individual Accountability Policy (I discussed this memo in the chapter on self-disclosures). The significance of the Yates Memo was that it revised

---

2 *In re Caremark International Inc. Derivative Litigation*, 698 A.2d 959 (Del. Ch. 1996).

the Principles of Corporate Prosecution to require that government attorneys pursue culpable individuals within an organization as part of their investigation and settlement process relating to corporate wrongdoing.

The memo requires that government attorneys investigate individuals as part of their investigation, whether it is a criminal or civil case, and that cases cannot be settled without such individuals being identified and a plan of action in place to pursue them. Corporations, likewise, must include investigations of individual accountability as part of their internal process and must disclose findings to the government investigators to secure credit for cooperating.

It is also important to note that board members and executives can be held responsible for corporate wrongdoing, even if they are not actually aware of it. Corporate officers can, in fact, be subject to conviction without proof of intent, negligence, or actual knowledge. The precedent for this goes back to the Park Doctrine, when the U.S. Supreme Court upheld an executive's misdemeanor conviction under the Food, Drug, and Cosmetic Act (FDCA).[3] The court, in this case, found that officers have a duty to prevent and remedy violations.

Note that the FDCA is a strict liability statute, where intent is not necessary for a violation. Another strict liability statute is the Stark Law, which does have

3 *United States v. Park*, 421 U.S. 658 (1975).

more relevance to a healthcare compliance officer. The point here is that corporate officers do have a duty of care, and that duty requires them to oversee the compliance program to ensure that sufficient information is provided to the board regarding compliance with laws, rules, and regulations.

Before you first meet with the board or board committee, meet with the CEO to gain insight into what to expect from that group and how best to present to them. You should be prepared to present an overview of why compliance programs exist, including references to the Federal Sentencing Guidelines and the OIG guidance documents, as well as evolving legal requirements such as the Deficit Reduction Act (DRA) and the Affordable Care Act (ACA), which have extinguished the "optional" aspect of compliance programs. Keep this portion of your presentation brief, because you don't want their attention to wander.

When you introduce the organization's compliance program, the best starting point is to outline the proposed structure of the program, including reporting relationships that may exist and the compliance plan document itself. If this is a new compliance program, ask the board to approve the compliance plan document, including the structure you are proposing to build. Inform them of the various reporting mechanisms that you have in place, or are proposing, and the auditing and monitoring processes. You should also be prepared to explain how you plan to identify risks in an ongoing manner and the process for addressing and reporting those risks.

Get the board involved in approving the Code of Conduct if it is new. The Code of Conduct establishes the foundation of Compliance, so you can't really move forward without agreement by the board, as mentioned previously.

You might be able to cover these foundational topics in one board meeting, or it may take more. You should report routinely to the board, whether quarterly, bimonthly, or on some other schedule. The ease with which you can get Compliance pieces approved can vary greatly, depending on the organization and board members. In some instances, I presented to the board, and they have then immediately approved everything. I have also presented to boards that got derailed by minor issues in the Code of Conduct (which in my mind were not even remotely controversial), causing delays in approvals. This can be frustrating, because you need the core documents approved before you can move on, but don't be disheartened; it is not unusual.

If you do run into unexpected delays or pushback from the board, you will likely have a debriefing with the CEO (if not, request one). Get feedback on your approach and insights for future presentations. Actually, it's a good idea to have this conversation regardless of how well presentations to the board go to strengthen your chances of success going forward and to ensure that you have a collaborative relationship with the CEO.

In addition to gaining support and approvals from the board, it is also your job to provide them with compliance education. Your first presentation that explains the background and genesis of compliance programs gets you started. My preference is to combine some education with regular updates at each report, including any current hot topics or industry developments that the board should be aware of.

You can accomplish education in tandem with reporting. You can summarize policies that you are implementing and give a brief background on each to educate board members on the various issues and why they need to be addressed. For instance, when you present the policy on financial arrangements, it is a good opportunity to educate the board about key government cases and scenarios the policy is intended to address.

As an aside, I am a believer in providing people (not just board members) with the answer to "Why are we doing this?" I think it greatly improves understanding and cooperation and establishes credibility in the role of the compliance officer.

Of course, you need to be sure that meetings with the board keep them abreast of relevant industry developments. If your board attendance is less frequent than you would like, it is particularly important to have clear and timely education included in your presentation. In the event of a government audit or investigation, it is critical to be able to demonstrate that you have educated your board.

Once you get past the introduction and program development phase, your reports should include routine auditing and monitoring activities and results, outcomes from items on your annual work plan initiatives, hotline and other incident-reporting summary-level information, and training and education activities. Include information on government audits and investigations and other significant issues that arise.

A key piece of information to learn about the board is how much detail they want. The CEO can help guide you, and look to past reports to this committee to gain a sense of the board's preferences. There is no point in reinventing the wheel if there is an existing framework. If it is a new committee, don't assume they will come armed with expectations for you. They may well ask you to tell them what they should be requesting! Be prepared with a summary-level outline of what your proposed board reports will include.

When you work on board reports, avoid bringing up topics that aren't significant or that are open questions. Making this distinction is a matter of judgment and experience. If a serious and credible allegation of fraud and abuse is leveled against the organization, you will be bringing in outside counsel and doing a large investigation, and the board will want to know about it immediately, even before the matter is resolved. A less significant matter, however, should not be brought to the board unless and until you have investigated and verified an actual problem exists. Then it is appropriate to report it, along with your corrective action plan. If you are in doubt, check with the CEO to avoid any missteps.

Be prepared to explain every nuance in your reports, and be able to provide the supporting documentation, if requested. The board may or may not be inclined to dive deep into the information you present. If you get a government investigation notice, for instance, you should bring the file to the board meeting so that you can respond to any questions members may ask. Know your hotline cases and the details of any audits, reviews, and other compliance activities, and always be prepared to explain how you are addressing any identified problems. Board meetings don't have to be a frightening experience, but you should understand and respect the importance of board members' role and be ready to provide them with the information they need.

A board member who is particularly well informed about laws, regulations, or current enforcement activities may surprise you. He or she may ask you about items that aren't in the report but that are in industry news. All you can do is be as prepared as possible. If you are asked about something that isn't in your report and that you are not familiar with, say you will certainly look into the issue and respond at the next meeting.

Of course, you never want to be in that situation; but if it happens, don't let it get you flustered, especially if you are in the middle of your presentation. Make sure that you fully understand what the person is asking, and then prepare a thorough understanding and response for the next meeting. If it is an issue that the board believes is pressing, they might expect your research and response sooner.

Just remember that their job, like yours, is to protect the company. If you can think of the board in that manner, presenting to them should be less intimidating. You have a great deal of responsibility in your role as compliance officer, and they are relying on you to help them do their duty.

As mentioned, a supportive board is useful when you encounter resistance from organizational leaders. Usually, when you can state truthfully that the board has reviewed and approved the initiative in question, it goes a long way toward reducing or eliminating resistance. Most leaders, regardless of how they feel about Compliance, know better than to go against a board-approved initiative.

A last comment about boards: I have actually seen board members fall asleep during a Compliance presentation, and I have presented to boards that grill me on details. When you consider taking on the role of compliance officer, it is a good idea to seek information about the board's engagement and interest in Compliance. My view is that it is better to have an actively involved board or board committee, even though it requires more of you, because it means the organization demonstrates commitment to Compliance at the highest levels.

# CONCLUSION

I HOPE THIS HANDBOOK HAS been useful and has provided helpful insights. My purpose is to share the operational lessons I have learned over the years that can help new compliance officers become aware of potential issues on the front end.

As I stated earlier, this is not a technical resource manual or legal advice, but I encourage you to locate those publications and the organizations that provide them to make sure that you understand the regulatory and technical requirements necessary for an effective compliance program. You need to be well versed in many laws and regulations, both at the federal and state levels, and these requirements change regularly.

Hone your researching skills. The more you become a trusted resource in the organization, the more you will be asked to weigh in on issues that aren't strictly compliance issues. Although that increases your workload, it is a very good sign that you have earned trust and respect across the organization.

One of the best things you can do is attend industry conferences so you can meet other compliance people and learn from them. Free compliance resources, such as groups on LinkedIn, are also available. You can sign up to get automatic emails from the Centers for Medicare and Medicaid Services and the Office of Inspector General; these can really help you keep informed of regulatory changes and enforcement trends. Don't be afraid to reach out to people with compliance experience if you get stuck or have a question; chances are good that someone else also has had the same question. Make use of online listservs and discussion groups and forums; you can put questions out there and hear from others so that everyone has the benefit of the answer. It's also a great way to network.

Healthcare compliance, to me, is a fascinating field of work, because it exists at the nexus of law and medicine, both constantly changing and evolving fields. It is a complex profession and is still growing, with many opportunities to expand your knowledge and skill set.

Good luck to you in all your endeavors, and feel free to find me on LinkedIn or on my website: compliancealacarte.com.

# ACKNOWLEDGEMENTS

I WOULD LIKE TO EXPRESS MY sincere appreciation to Alton Knight, Bonnie Rodriguez, and Misty Bridwell, for the time spent reviewing and providing input on early versions of this book. Their ideas and suggestions were invaluable, and I am grateful for their efforts. In addition to these individuals, I feel fortunate to have had an interesting array of professional opportunities over the years, as well as contact with many talented individuals and unique situations that have made my career a fascinating ride so far!

Made in the USA
Coppell, TX
30 April 2025

48883681R00173